CHRISTMAS MAN

Also by Harold Davis

The Starrigans of Little Brook Bottom

CHRISTMAS MAN

Harold Davis

ISBN: 0994838816
ISBN 13: 9780994838810

For Sharon

Happy, happy Christmas, that can win us back to the delusions of our childish days; that can recall to the old man the pleasures of his youth; that can transport the sailor and the traveller, thousands of miles away, back to his own fire-side and his quiet home!"

— Charles Dickens

NAPPER

John Albert Darby died just after sun-up on the twenty-eighth of December. He was eighty-seven and likely pleased with the timing of his departure. Waiting any longer would have interfered with a new year while getting away earlier would have marred Christmas—an intolerable notion for sure.

I mention Christmas for good reason when I speak of Napper. The truth is you would have a hard time saying his name to anyone here in John's Pond without a reference being made to the great season. (Oh, please understand, John Albert Darby and Napper Darby were one and the same person although he used his proper name only about as often as he used the christening gown he wore to get it.) Christmas you see, more than any other piece of the year, plants notions of joy and cheer to linger in our minds. For some it is images of bright lights and gaily-wrapped gifts. For others it is memories of perfect trees and music that has stirred the human spirit for centuries. Many still keep the blessed origin of the feast in mind. Here, in John's Pond, Christmas will always conjure up stories of Napper, the Christmas Man; he lived right here among us.

I remember him. Not well, mind you. The last ten Christmases of Napper Darby's life were the first ten of mine and I have enjoyed a good many since. How did Napper come to be known as the Christmas Man you ask? It isn't easy to explain. Many things, one piled on top of the other, made him what he was and I doubt if any one person knows all of it but I will tell you a few bits and pieces that are familiar to the young and old around here. It will help you understand why he still warms our hearts on Christmas Day.

There was little sign of the Christmas spirit or any other benevolence when Napper was born on a grey Wednesday morning in March 1881. The dozen houses that made up the village of John's Pond lay hodgepodge around the mouth of Rocky River on Newfoundland's foggy south coast. During the brief summers the livyers caught salmon in the river and codfish in the bay. They planted potatoes, carrots and turnips in gardens behind their houses and foraged for berries on the barrens. In wintertime they trapped fur, cut firewood and longed for spring. Nobody in the place was prosperous but with hard work and economy the people eked a living from the woods and water. The quality of that living varied from house to house but in one unpainted shanty, squat out of sight behind the village, it rarely rose above misery. It was the home of Cecil and Lilly Darby and, with Napper's arrival, five youngsters.

Nobody celebrated his birth. His mother dozed to escape for as long as possible the worry of feeding another mouth. Cecil sat by the stove shifting his gaze between the sleet pelting against the window and the near-empty wood-box. He avoided the eyes of his youngsters in the kitchen; they, in turn, ignored him—directing their occasional mutterings to each other. As soon as it was decent to do so after bringing Napper into the world the midwife lit out for her own place. The northeast wind pushed her along.

"Some people should never be allowed to have youngsters," she said to her husband when she was able to warm herself by her own kitchen stove. "Those poor little things are over in that shack in their bare feet. I'm sure they never had a decent meal in two weeks."

"It mightn't be as bad as it looks. Lil's been laid up on account of having the baby."

"Don't talk so foolish. There's no reason he can't keep the house and young ones clean. Soap and water is easy to come by. He's useless."

"It'll all work out."

"No thanks to that layabout if it does."

Some say nature took its course. Others say heaven ends all misery. What you believe doesn't matter. A week after she brought Napper into the world Lilly Darby passed from it. Napper and his brothers and sisters were left to make their way through childhood in a home with nothing. But against the odds, and with hand-outs from heaven and neighbours, they survived. When he was six years old Napper's life was shoved in a new direction.

The change began with David Thistle showing up from St. John's. He had big plans, pockets full of money and had gotten wind of the vast stands of timber upriver from John's Pond. Almost before the residents realised it a steam-powered sawmill stood among them belching smoke into the sky and screaming for logs and millworkers. Newcomers arrived to work in the mill and they brought their families with them. That created the need for a new school.

Up to then John's Pond had been making do with visiting teachers who rarely stayed more than two months of the year. When a teacher was available the scholars of the place all fit into Mrs. Lizzie Fleming's front room. Since the teacher boarded with

Mrs. Lizzie and her husband, Mr. Mike, the arrangement was convenient and satisfactory. But now Mrs. Lizzie's front room just wasn't up to the task.

In early December of the same year that Mr. Thistle established his sawmill all hands got together in a kitchen meeting. They agreed to cut a thousand logs—two days work for ten men—when they went in the woods after Christmas. Five hundred logs would be sawed into lumber to build the school; the other five hundred would be sold to get money for nails, window-glass and a stove. Things went more or less as planned and by the following June a tidy little schoolhouse stood on the hill near the bridge. Recruiting a teacher was another matter but by writing a letter to the bishop and sending a petition to the government a suitable candidate was found. Like her predecessors she boarded with Mr. Mike and Mrs. Lizzie.

SCHOOL-TIME CHRISTMAS

Judy Power knew when she agreed to come to John's Pond that she would not have the amenities of a school in the city but she never expected the likes of this—thirty-one children from age six to fifteen. A handful were clean, well-fed and well-dressed. Most of the others were clean and well fed. A few could only claim to be clean. The rest were Darbys. Billy, thirteen, sat in a corner at the back of the classroom and said nothing. Cecil, a year younger, sat in the corner opposite and, if it was possible, said less. Margaret, who went as Peggy, was ten, while Hannah was eight. The two girls shared a table and played together at recess. None of the other children were disposed to taking the place of either one.

"I'm sure they are pretty little things," Judy wrote to her mother, "if only I could see past the dirt." The youngest Darby in the class according the register was John Albert. "You should see him, mother. Everyone calls him Napper. He tells me it's because he slept a lot but that's hard to believe. He doesn't stop talking long enough to sleep."

Her first encounter with Napper was engraved in her memory. She was determined on her first day not to be overwhelmed by the rag-tag class.

"My name is Miss Power. I want to get to know all of you as soon as I can. We will begin by each of you telling me your name, your age and what you like best about school. We'll start—"

"I'm Napper. I like that picture." He was pointing to the coloured world map the teacher had hung on the wall.

"You must wait until I tell you to speak before you say anything. You mustn't—"

"You told us to say our names and what we liked. That's what you said. That's what she said isn't it, Peggy?"

His sister's face reddened and Judy was afraid the little girl might bolt for the door. She patted her on the shoulder to let her know everything was all right and then looked at Napper.

"Shush, for a minute and listen to me. If you want to speak in school you must raise your hand. I'll tell you when it's OK to talk. Do you understand?"

Napper's hand shot up.

"That's better. Now, please tell me your name again."

"Napper."

"How old are you, Napper?"

"Six. How old are you?"

"I'm older than you. Tell me, do you think you will like school?"

"I don't know. Our old man says he can't see it doing any damn good."

Judy got her classroom under control but said nothing more to him until he was leaving the classroom with the others at the end of the day. "Napper, will you help me with some of my books?"

"All right." He turned and came to her desk. Buttons were missing from his brown shirt—a shirt that was too big by several sizes. Someone lacking skill or care, perhaps both, had constructed his coarse wool pants. They were dirty and too big. His boots had numerous repairs and needed more. He smiled at her.

"Which ones do you want me to carry?"

"I'll get them for you. You look like you had fun today. Are you going to come back tomorrow?"

"Yep. I liked that story you told about the whale."

"You were supposed to be doing your printing when we were reading that."

"I had it finished. That stuff is easy. Hannah and Peggy showed me how to do it when I was small."

The teacher scanned the skinny child. "I see. What else did they teach you?"

"I think I can read a bit and I can print my name."

"Really? You're going to do well in school but you must be careful about things you say."

"Like today when everybody laughed at me?"

"That's right. Language like that makes you look silly. That's why everyone laughed. They knew you weren't supposed to say it."

"I figured I did something wrong. I won't do it again Miss, no matter what the old man says."

Napper was true to his word and never made the mistake of using bad language again. That's not to say it was all clear sailing; it wasn't. Like the time one chilly morning he gathered rinds from around the wood box and threw them in the stove to get the fire going better. He was hardly back in his seat when the dampers and chimney funnels blasted off the stove. He might have been blamed for stashing the firecrackers in the rinds except Calvin Squires was laughing so hard he started to snort. But apart from a scattered snarl like that school was a great adventure for young Napper. He soaked in every word Judy Power spoke to his class and most of what she said to the students in the other grades. The teacher noted his enthusiasm.

"He's as bright as a button," she wrote in one of her weekly letters to her mother. "It's a shame he doesn't have a better chance of making something of his life. I hope the time I spend here makes things a little better for him."

Winter came early that year. A foot of snow covered the ground by the first week of December. Napper's breath drifted like smoke in the morning air and the snow scrunched under his feet as he followed Billy's tracks across the meadow towards the schoolhouse. It was Billy's turn to light the fire in the school and he left the house as soon as he finished his share of the porridge and washed it down with black tea. Napper lingered to soak in as much heat as he could until he finally had to go. The cold air stung his cheeks and made his nose run. Two horses pulling slides passed him as they trotted towards the woods. Their harness bells tinkled in the still air. He met Miss Power at the bottom of the schoolhouse hill. Her arms were full.

"Good morning, Napper. Don't those bells make you think about Christmas?"

"I suppose."

"They sound wonderful to me. They remind me how busy everybody gets this time of the year."

Napper's quizzical glance told her that the youngster didn't relate to what she knew to be the sights, sounds and even smells of Christmas. By now her mother had the house scrubbed from bottom to top and enough cakes and pastries baked to feed a multitude of visitors. Her sisters would have badgered their father into bringing down the boxes of decorations from the attic so they could sort through them—replacing anything tattered with something new and sparkling from the Water Street shops.

"Do you want me to carry some of those bags for you, Miss?"

"Thank you, Napper. That will be a big help." She passed him two of the bulky packages.

"What's in them?"

"Oh, just a few things mother sent me to put up in the school."

"What kind of things?"

"Christmas things. Can you keep a secret?" she asked even though she knew it was impossible for him.

"That's no problem for me, Miss."

"I want to make this a special Christmas for everybody in the school so we're ending classes early today and we're going to decorate the schoolhouse. Mother sent me lots of tinsel, crepe paper, strings and beads that we can use."

"Wow! Can I do some?"

"Of course, but don't tell anyone yet. I want it to be a surprise."

"I won't. I'm going to go on ahead and see if Billy got the fire lit. I'll see you in the school."

"OK."

She laughed as he hustled up the hill, strealing the bulky bags along with him. She knew that word of her plans would be spread through the schoolyard before she got near the place.

Once inside the schoolhouse she stashed all the bags in a corner behind her desk. Billy had a fire crackling in the pot-bellied stove and was gone back outside to skylark with the other boys while they waited for class to start. Napper was still inside. Heat began to radiate from the stove but it would still be an hour before the room could be called warm. Judy left on her coat as she sorted her day's work. Napper took off his mitts and smacked them across the stove half a dozen times to knock off the snow. The pungent odour of burning wool reached the teacher but before she could tell him to stop he tossed the mitts under the stove to dry. Then he opened the stove door and piled three or four spruce junks on top of the kindling.

"Won't take long to warm up now, Miss."

"Thank you, Napper," she said. Then, without looking at him, she asked, "How does your family celebrate Christmas?"

"Sometimes we have a big dinner. Last year Mr. Dickie Croke gave us a quarter of mutton. We had gravy and a pile of potatoes with it. Most of the time the old man gets at the homebrew and ends up in the staggers and jags. He starts singing but he hasn't got a note in his head."

She kept her face turned away from him. Memories of Christmases from her own childhood raced through her mind. Her father was prominent in all of them—a gentleman presiding over feasts and gifts with warmth and joy—the essence of benevolence. She took a deep breath and forced a smile before she faced the waif again.

"Well, I'm sure you'll enjoy what I have planned. I think it will put you right in the spirit of the season."

The students were unsettled throughout the day. They paid as much attention to the bags in the corner as they did to the teacher. She said nothing of her plans but it was obvious from the activity around Napper that he kept the secret no longer than she expected. The students were not disappointed. Instead of starting classes in the afternoon she stood in front of them and smiled.

"I want everyone to put away your slate-boards and push the benches in by the wall. Pull three or four tables together in the middle of the room so we can spread out some stuff I brought for us."

As soon as they had room to work, she began to take the supplies out of the bags. The faces of the children confirmed that they were accustomed to smaller quantities and lower qualities of Christmas decorations. She showed them how to make paper snowflakes, and how to criss-cross green and red crepe paper to make box streamers. The streamers were stretched from one corner of the schoolroom to the other. About an hour into the operation sleigh-bells were heard in the yard.

"It's Mr. Mike Fleming," one of the children said. "He's got a tree on the slide. What's he doing with that, Miss?"

"We're putting up a Christmas tree."

"What's a Christmas tree, Miss?"

"What do we do with it, Miss?"

"We're going to bring it in here and decorate it. Just watch and see." The children were pressed against the window watching Mike Fleming untie the tree. "Some houses in St. John's have been putting them up over the last few years. It will be tremendous fun. You'll like it."

The youngsters ran to the door as Mike Fleming hauled the tree to the schoolhouse entrance. It was huge—ten feet high and almost as wide. The older boys tugged it in through the door while the girls scrambled to clear a path. The smallest children stared, wide-eyed, at the huge ornament in their midst.

"What a size, Miss!"

"Miss, where will we put it?"

"How can we decorate the top, Miss? It's too big."

"Miss, is there enough room for it?"

"Wait, wait, wait. One at a time, please! Oh my, it is a little larger than I expected."

As big as the tree was, all the eager hands had it decorated in minutes. A galvanized bucket was filled with sand and used as a tree-stand. Smiles lit every face as the students admired their creation. The teacher told them that one more thing was needed.

"We're going to have to make a star to go on the top of it," she said. "Does anyone know how to make a perfect one?" Nobody stepped forward. "Ok, then. I'll show you. Come over here by the blackboard." They followed her like chicks behind a hen. She picked up a wooden instrument from her desk. "Does anybody remember what this is?"

"A compass?" one girl offered.

"That's right. What do we use it for?"

"Drawing circles!"

"OK, let's draw one." She picked up a wide, flat board from the corner where the decorations had been. "Somebody hold this so everyone can see it." One of the older girls stepped forward and held the board as instructed. The teacher drew a circle on it. She then laid down the compass and picked up another implement. "What's this?"

"A tractor," one of the senior girls said.

"A *pro*tractor," Miss Power said. "What do we use it for?"

"Measuring degrees," said voice from the other side of the room.

"That's right. Now I need to know how many points there are on a star."

"Five!"

"Six!"

"Eight!"

"Stop! Stop! Stop!" she laughed. "Maybe all of you are right but we'll have five points on our star. Now, how many degrees there are in a circle?"

"Three hundred and sixty," one older student said.

"That's right. So if we have five points on our star and they are all the same distance apart, that means we have a point at every seventy-two degrees. Like this, see?" She measured each point on the circle drawn on the board. "Now, all we have to do is join the points like this, and we have a perfect star that we can cut out and paint. I will ask Mr. Mike to cut this one out for us tonight and we can put it on the tree tomorrow."

I heard Napper Darby himself say more than eighty years later that the like of the Christmas tree they raised in the schoolhouse that day was never seen since. Glorious, he said it was, just glorious. He also said that was the day when it dawned on him that

Christmas was a wondrous time unlike any other time of the year. Over eighty years and he never forgot it—nor did he forget the geometry lesson Judy Power taught that day to a schoolhouse full of youngsters who thought they had gotten out of class early.

There was no problem with school attendance for the next two weeks. Not only did the students show up, but just about everyone else in the place also paid a visit. They came to be dazzled by the beauty created by the teacher and her students. A concert was held in the school the night before the Christmas holidays started. Napper and his classmates sang their hearts out. Some of the adults also took part. Mike Fleming recited *The Little Dream That Saved*. Others sang songs that had been sung in John's Pond since the first roof was raised there. Everyone agreed though, the highlight of the evening was Miss Power singing *The First Noel*.

"I'll be seventy-nine next May if God spares me," old Matt Nowlan was heard to say as he left the building, "and I never heard the likes of it in all my days."

Mike and Lizzie Fleming waited while the last of the concert-goers congratulated and thanked Judy. Finally they were able to leave the schoolhouse. Mike tied the door shut with some trawl twine.

"That'll stop the wind from blowing it open until you come back in January," he said.

The three of them chatted and laughed as they made their way down from the school-house hill and along the lanes to home. Judy couldn't get the smile off her face. She was tired, but her work was done and tomorrow she was going home for the holidays!

CHRISTMAS SNOW

The next morning, as Judy snuggled deep under the quilts piled on her bed, a dull roar worked its way into her slumber. It seemed to shake her bed. Slowly she realised the bed and the rest of the house was shaking.

"Oh, no! No, not today!" She bolted from the bed and fell towards the window. She knew before she could scrape the frost from the windowpane what she would see. The world outside was white chaos. Gusting winds slammed snow against the house. The fence was almost buried and she couldn't see the road, but it didn't matter; nobody would be travelling today. She sat back on her bed and tried to stop the panic rising within her. Today was the twenty-second. The storm would last all day and perhaps tomorrow. The roads were blocked and it would be days, maybe a week, before paths could be beaten through the snowdrifts enabling passage to the city.

Her Christmas would be spent in John's Pond.

Mike and Lizzie Fleming were waiting at the kitchen table when she came downstairs.

"Sit down my love," Mrs. Lizzie said. She put her arms around the red-eyed young woman and led her to a chair. "I have some toast in the warmer and I'll make you a nice cup of tea." Judy sniffled as she took her chair.

"I know you must be heart-broken," Mr. Mike said, "but I've always found that things have a way working out for the best."

"You don't think there's any chance of me getting home, do you?"

"No, my darling" he said. "It's likely to be a week or longer before the road is passable."

"Oh, why did this have to happen now? I can't believe I'm not going to get home for Christmas."

Tears streamed down Judy's face as Mrs. Lizzie laid a steaming mug of tea and two thick slices of toast in front of her. The elderly woman put her arms around her and stroked her hair.

"Don't you worry," the old woman said. "You're going to have a good Christmas. I know you'd sooner be home but folks around here think the world of you and they're going to make sure you enjoy your time with us."

"It's not that I don't like it here. I do. It's just that I was looking forward so much to seeing mother and father and my sisters and now…" She could no longer control her sobs. Mrs. Lizzie stood her up and embraced her. Judy buried her face on the old woman's shoulder and let her tears flow.

"There, there, my love. It's going to be all right. You go right ahead and cry as long as you need." The old woman hugged Judy tightly as she sobbed on her shoulder. After a few minutes the young woman straightened up. She tried to dry the tears from her red face with the heel of her hand.

"I'm sorry. I shouldn't be such a baby, especially when everyone is so good to me."

Mrs. Lizzie handed her a cloth to wipe her face and then encouraged her to sit to the table again. "You'll feel better after you have a cup of tea."

Still sniffling, Judy nodded. Her hands trembled as she removed the cover from the sugar dish and lifted out a spoonful of sugar. She stirred the sugar into her tea and reached for the milk jug but before she could get it Mike Fleming leaned forward and wrapped his huge leathery paw around her hand.

"Can you take some advice from an old fool?"

"He's well qualified to give it," his wife said from where she stood by the stove.

Judy laughed through her sniffles as the old man continued. "My father used to say, 'Force put is no man's choice.' He was dead ten years before I figured out what he was getting on with. He was saying there are things we can't control so we have to make the best of them. You're facing one of them now."

"I can't do much about a blizzard. That's for sure."

"True enough. But you can make up your own mind what you do with yourself and from what I've seen of you I'd say we can expect this to be a Christmas like no other."

"What do you mean?"

"I'm not sure but it was only two or three nights ago that myself and Lizzie were saying how grand it would be to have you with us for Christmas and lo and behold—here you are."

"You think it was meant that I should stay here?"

"All things are for a reason my girl. I don't know why this happened to you but something tells me we're all going to be better off for it."

"Mr. Mike, you know I adore you and Mrs. Lizzie. You're like another mother and father to me. It's just that I was looking forward so much to being home." Her voice started to break again. Mrs. Lizzie walked across the kitchen and stood behind Judy's chair. She leaned over and kissed the girl on the cheek.

"Your mom and dad are going to be worried about you. Why don't you eat your breakfast and then get dressed and go see when

Dick Croke is going to Whitbourne for the mail. He can send a telegram to your parents so they'll know you're all right."

"I suppose I should. I may as well make it official." She forced a laugh.

"Good girl," Mrs. Lizzie said. "It might be a lot to ask but I think you should try to make it sound happy. Your parents won't enjoy their Christmas if they think you're miserable out here."

"I'll remind them I'm in good hands." She smiled across the table at Mr. Mike and then stood up and hugged his wife. "I've written them so often and told them how good you are to me that they might think I didn't want to come home."

"Oh, they'll know different from that my sweet," Mike said, "but I have to tell you the truth, I'm some happy we have you here with us. Get dressed nice and warm when you're ready. I'll walk down to Dickie's with you so you don't blow away."

About an hour later, linked arm and arm with Mr. Mike, she made her way through the blizzard towards Dick Croke's house. The wind and snow swirled around them and she clung to the old man as the gusts threatened to sweep her off her feet. She was surprised to see so many people out and about. Men were shovelling the snow from their doorways and bringing in firewood to fill the wood-boxes in the kitchens. They met a couple of women making their way towards Thistle's store and paused to exchange observations about the storm with them but it was the number of children on the go that Judy marvelled at.

"I expected everyone to stay indoors today." She had to yell to be heard over the storm.

"And miss the fun?" Mr. Mike yelled back.

"What fun?"

He pulled her into the lee of a spruce grove. "Look around." He pointed at three youngsters somersaulting from the top rail of a fence into a snowdrift. Not far from them four more were digging a cave into a drift. A couple of snowmen were under construction but it was the activity on the schoolhouse hill that got the old man grinning from ear to ear. "Look! They have a hand-cat."

"A what?"

"A hand-cat—that big sled. Watch them come down the hill. That thing will go like a bullet."

Judy watched the boys and girls. She also saw how the grin didn't leave Mr. Mike's face as he gazed at the young ones. At least seven children were involved in the exercise of pushing and pulling the huge sled to the top of the steepest and longest part of the hill. Once there the biggest boy held the hand-cat in place while the rest piled on. Judy's curiosity turned to alarm.

"They aren't all getting on that thing are they?"

"Oh yes," Mr. Mike said, "indeed they are."

Before Judy said anything else the boy holding the hand-cat pushed it over the edge. He chased it as it gathered speed. When he could barely keep up with it he jumped on the back runners. Judy could hear the squeals of the children above the gale as the hand-cat careened down the hill. It plunged down the steepest part of the slope and across a small meadow at the bottom where the boy on the back threw his weight sideways turning the sled onto the road. It came barrelling towards Judy and Mr. Mike until, just in front of them, the young fellow on the back turned it sideways again spilling the riders into the snow. One of the first to recover and pop up was young Napper.

"Hey, Miss! I thought you were gone to St. John's. Do you want a ride? It's fun."

"I don't think I'm ready to ride on that thing yet, Napper."

The boy who had piloted the hand-cat down the hill spoke up. "It's OK, Miss. I don't go fast." It was Napper's older brother.

"It's too fast for me, Cecil. I'll stick to walking." She couldn't help but laugh as one child after another picked itself up out of the snow. They looked like some kind of snow people smiling back at her.

"Are you staying here for Christmas, Miss?" Napper asked.

"It looks that way, Napper. I'm on my way to ask Mr. Dick Croke to send a telegram to my parents for me."

"Mr. Dickie is in the store," Napper said, pointing towards Thistle's Store. "I saw him going in there a few minutes ago." The youngsters had the sled up-righted again and were ready to haul it back up the hill.

"Come on, Miss. Take one ride with us."

She laughed and shook her head. "Maybe I'll be brave enough later. I have to see Mr. Croke now."

The youngsters waved to Judy as they started back up the hill. She turned to Mike, "I'd be scared to death on that thing."

"Don't talk so foolish," he said. "When I was a young fellow I came down that hill ten thousand times on a hand-cat and loved every trip. I'd do it again today only for Lizzie would have a fit. Come on. Let's find Dickie and get that message to your folks."

Dick Croke was about fifty years old: long, lanky and loud. He had been a trapper for most of his adult life but for the last ten years he earned a living 'running the mail'. Twice a week, all through the year, he trekked to the train station in Whitbourne to pick up the incoming mail and drop off whatever was going out. It was more than thirty miles round trip. He used a horse and carriage or sleigh when he could, but he walked when the road was impassable for a horse-drawn vehicle. A lot of mail came and went on his back. Along with his postal duties Dick ran all sorts of errands. On any day he might be carrying medicine, horseshoes or even dry goods for some of the John's Pond women. One wry male resident observed that, 'Dickie Croke decides what women are the best dressed around here.' His travels and passion for spinning a yarn made him the primary supplier of news. It was in that capacity

Mike Fleming and the young teacher found him when they walked into Thistle's store. Eight or nine men and women surrounded him. He wound up his story to greet the newcomers.

"How are you doing, Mike? I see you traded Lizzie for something newer. I'd say you got the best part of the deal." He took off his cap and extended his hand to Judy. "My dear, someone as lovely as yourself should have held out for better than this old goat. How are you?" Everyone in the store laughed. Judy laughed along with them.

"Mr. Croke, you are scandalous and you're wrong. I think Mr. Mike would be a fine catch for any woman." The crowd laughed again as Mike Fleming put his arm around Judy and winked at Dickie who was not about to let someone else have the last word.

"Miss, I know you're the school teacher and I don't mean to be questioning my betters but that's not snow on the top of his head."

Judy waited for the laughter to settle before speaking again. "Mr. Croke, do you think you'll be able to get to Whitbourne anytime soon?"

"I dare say I'll be able to punch my way through sometime tomorrow. Why? You're not planning on coming with me are you?"

"No, I can't keep up with you. I want to ask you to send this telegram to my parents for me." She passed him a folded piece of paper. He opened it and whispered the words as he read.

BLIZZARD. ALL ROADS BLOCKED. SPENDING CHRISTMAS WITH FLEMINGS. SAFE AND HAPPY. MERRY CHRISTMAS TO ALL. LOVE JUDY.

He looked at Judy while he folded the note and put it in his pocket. He delivered many telegrams over the years. Sometimes they held good news; usually it was bad—often the death of a loved one. He knew the few terse words never conveyed all the emotions behind them.

"I have to get there and back by Christmas Eve. I'll make sure this gets sent. Don't you worry your mind about it."

"Thank you." She opened her handbag. "How much will it cost to send it? It's seventeen words."

"Not a copper. There'll be no peace on Earth for Sparkie this Christmas if he tries to charge me. Not after all the berries and salmon I've brought to him."

"Are you sure?"

"I'm sure. You keep your money. I'll look after this."

"Thank you very much. I know they're going to be worrying about me."

"You're in good hands. Now, will you promise to do something for me?"

"Of course. What is it?"

"Make sure you come by my house during Christmas."

"Mine too," someone else said before she could answer.

"And ours," said another.

Requests to visit came at Judy from all sides. She laughed as she said, "I'll do my very best to see as many people as I can."

"But she can't be everywhere," Mike Fleming said. He stepped up behind Judy put his hands on her shoulders and pulled her close to him. "She's on her holidays and I don't want to see her running all around the place trying to make sure no one gets vexed because she didn't get to their house."

"Oh, Mr. Mike," she said, "you worry about me too much. That won't happen."

"Oh yes, indeed it will," Dickie Croke said. "I'll be the first to start a row if you don't come around to see me and the missus, and that old man behind you can't do anything about it."

Judy laughed and stepped up to the outlandish mailman. She took his hands in hers. "Mr. Croke, you can count on two visitors this Christmas and I'm one of them."

"Who's the other one?"

"Why St. Nicholas, of course!"

"That's right. I forgot all about him." Dickie put on his cap and looked at the crowd. "All of you mind what you heard here this morning. When you're good, like I am, Father Christmas and pretty women will always be looking out for you." With that, and amid laughter and wisecracks, he made his exit.

"What is he like at all?" one of the women in the store said as Dickie disappeared into the storm.

"He's a character all right," a man said, "but nobody else would ever make that trip in some of the weather he does." Their attention returned to Judy.

"You must be disappointed not to be going home for Christmas?" one said.

"I was but I'm getting over it. I love it here and it will be different than Christmas in the city."

"A lot different, I'd say."

"The important stuff about Christmas is the same everywhere, good friends, good times and the blessed reason behind it all. Lots of things are the same when you think about it."

"Maybe, but I'd like to spend one Christmas in St. John's. I'd love to see those new electric lights I heard they put in the stores."

"The lights are nice but only a few stores on Water Street have them. Besides, if you walked into those stores people wouldn't be inviting you to their homes like you've been doing to me. I think that's a lot nicer than any lights."

Mike Fleming beamed as he listened to Judy. It was hard to believe this was the same distraught young woman who was sitting at his kitchen table a short while earlier. He caught her attention.

"Well my dear, unless you need something else, how about we start making our way back to the house? Lizzie promised to have fish cakes for lunch and I know she got partridgeberry crumble looking for   praise.

Judy said her good-byes to the people in the store and holding tightly to Mike's arm ventured out into the storm again. She felt much better than she did earlier. As they walked along the road she turned to him.

"I have a wonderful idea," she said.

Lizzie Fleming stared out her kitchen window at the two figures staggering in the lane from the road. She knew it was her husband and Judy but they were doubled over and taking both sides of the path. For a second she thought something was wrong with one of them. Then she saw they were laughing hard. She met them at the porch door.

"Look at the mess of snow on you. What in heaven's name happened to the two of you?"

"We were, we were..." The old man couldn't stop laughing. "We were...you tell her," he said to Judy.

"Oh, Mrs. Lizzie," Judy fell back against the porch wall laughing so hard she could barely get the words out, "we were riding on a hand-cat!"

Both of them collapsed in laughter again.

"Get in here you old fool before everyone in the place sees you. Are you trying to ruin Judy's good name?"

"It was her idea. I didn't even want to do it—"

"A likely story."

"—but she talked me into it."

"You're the one who told me how much fun it was," Judy said. Tears of laughter ran down her face. "I was afraid to go by myself."

"One of you is worse than the other," Mrs. Lizzie said. "Come in here and get yourselves tidied up while I get your lunch ready. What would the school-children ever think if they saw Judy riding on a hand-cat?"

"But, Mrs. Lizzie, it was the children's hand-cat that we used. Mr. Mike gave them five cents to haul it up to the top of the hill for us!"

Lizzie turned to her husband but he put his hand on her shoulder and held her at bay. "Now, now, my love. Don't be cross. I only paid them once to haul it up. They did it for nothing the other two times!"

CHRISTMAS FRIENDS

It was late on the evening of the twenty-third before the storm finally abated. Judy, free from the tests and lessons of the schoolhouse, was able to enjoy her time with the Flemings. She helped Mrs. Lizzie bake one last Christmas cake, marvelling at how the old woman worked from memory, using recipes passed by word of mouth through generations. Mr. Mike puttered about keeping the stove and wood-box full. He was a gifted storyteller and fascinated Judy with tales from the earliest days in John's Pond. It amazed her that a place so wild existed so close to her home in the city.

On Christmas Eve Mrs. Lizzie looked out the window to see a child coming in the lane. "I believe it's one of the Darby youngsters isn't it, Mike?"

"That it is. It's young Napper. I told him to come over and I'd give him some mitts."

"What mitts are you giving him?"

"These," he said, holding up a pair.

"But I only knit them for you this fall."

"I know but he needs them more than me. The ones he had on his hands riding on the hand-cat the other day are full of holes."

Napper opened the door and walked into the kitchen.

"Come in, young fellow," Mike said. "Merry Christmas to you."

"Merry Christmas, Mr. Mike and to you too Mrs. Lizzie," he said. He smiled at Judy. "Merry Christmas, Miss."

"Thank you, Napper and Merry Christmas to you," she said.

"Would you like a piece of cake and a glass of syrup?" Mrs. Lizzie asked the child.

"Yeah," he said.

His ear-to-ear grin told Judy it was a rare treat. He pulled out a chair and sat to the table. Mike leaned back in a chair across the table from him.

"Have you got a girlfriend yet?"

"No."

"Why not?"

"I don't want one."

"Don't want one? How old are you?"

"Almost seven."

"Almost seven and no girlfriend. I don't know what's wrong with you young fellows today. When I was your age I had two or three girlfriends."

"Mrs. Lizzie…"

"If he did child, I knew nothing about it." She stirred a dollop of strawberry syrup into a tumbler of cold water and then put the syrup and a slice of dark fruitcake in front of Napper. "You eat your cake and pay him no mind." She clucked her tongue at her husband. "Can't you act your age for once in your life?"

"Ah, maybe that's it. You don't want anyone telling you what to do. You're too smart to get tangled up with women, aren't you? "

"Yep," he said through a mouthful of cake.

"I'll tell you what I'll do. Seeing as how you have neither girl-friend to keep you warm I'll give you a pair of wool socks to go along with them mitts. How's that?"

Mrs. Lizzie gagged on the raisin bun she was eating. Judy low-ered her head to stifle her giggles.

"Wow, socks and mitts! Thanks Mr. Mike. Thanks Mrs. Lizzie. Do you want to go riding on the hand-cat again today, Miss?"

"Not today, Napper," Judy said, "but if you have time you can help me."

"OK. What do you want me to do?"

"Well, I would like to visit some people. I know most of them but I'm not sure who lives in which house. Would you be good enough to come with me?"

"Would I ever!" The smile on his face couldn't get any wider. The Flemings and Judy knew that in a split second he figured out that accompanying the teacher pretty much guaranteed him a treat at every house they visited. "When do you want to start, Miss?"

Mike cut in before Judy could reply. "It's going to take Miss Power a little while to get ready. You'll find as you get older that women are slower getting ready than us men. Liz, seeing as how this young fellow is good enough to give up his day to look after Miss Power, why don't you cut off another chunk of cake for him to eat while he's waiting?"

Napper grinned.

OUT AND ABOUT AT CHRISTMAS

Judy Power set out from the Flemings' house late in the morning. Napper was at her side. She wasn't sure how she was going to approach visiting strange homes unannounced and uninvited. She was leery of Mike's instructions, "Never mind knocking. Open the doors and go on in. Everyone knows you." She planned to call on one, maybe two, families before lunch. If it appeared that she was welcomed she would continue with the visits in the afternoon.

Napper suggested that they go to the last house and work their way back. Ambrose and Nellie Critch lived there. They were a young couple with one child in school and two more at home. Judy was nervous as she approached the house but young Napper had his own protocol. As they stepped off the road onto the path leading to the Critch's door he bolted ahead of the teacher and ran into the porch.

"Mr. Ambrose! Mrs. Nellie! The teacher coming to see you!"

Judy's apprehension grew as she heard Nellie Critch's voice. "Oh my heavens, Ambrose, she is. Wipe off the table. Pick up that stuff off the floor." Nellie was untying her apron as she appeared in the door. "Miss Power, please come in. I can't believe you came to see us."

"If it's an inconvenient time I can come again later."

"Oh no, Miss Power," Ambrose said as he joined his wife. "Come in, come in. Please. Sit down over here by the stove."

"I'll put the kettle on for you, Miss Power," Nellie said. "Can I take your coat? Ambrose, get the fruitcake from the pantry."

Judy smiled at them and at the children peeping out from the next room.

"Mr. and Mrs. Critch, before you go to any trouble may I ask a favour of you?"

"Yes, anything, Miss Power. What can we do for you?"

"Stop fussing over me and please call me Judy. Only the children call me Miss Power."

The couple looked at each other. After a few seconds he said, "If that's what you want but we always called the teacher 'Miss'."

"When was the last time a teacher came to visit you?"

"Oh, you're the first," Nellie said. "I can't get over you being here."

Judy got up from her chair by the stove and took each of them by the arm. She led them to the kitchen table where she indicated they should all sit down. "How old are you?" she asked.

"I'm twenty-five," he said. "Nellie is twenty-three."

"I'm nineteen," Judy said. "You're way ahead of me. You have a home and a beautiful family..."

By the time Judy took her leave more than an hour later she knew all about the economies required to build a house, had dressed the Critch's four-month-old baby and endeared herself to new friends forever.

The second home she visited belonged to Will and Mae Kerrivan. Judy kept a grip on Napper until she was able to knock

on the door. Will opened it and immediately admonished her, "…
don't be so foolish, knocking. Everyone knows you. Come on in."

They were in their mid-forties and although they had eight
children only three were still in school; the others were grown and
as Will explained, "out on their own". As at the previous house,
Judy was treated like royalty and was only able to beg her way out
by assuring them that she would make every effort to visit again
during Christmas.

Throughout the afternoon Napper led her to four more homes
until at about four o'clock they were at the lane that lead to Mrs.
Maude O'Grady's door. Napper didn't seem as eager to go inside
this house. Judy suspected his craving for sweets was satisfied. He
said that nobody wanted to go there—a statement that caused a little bit of unease for Judy as she knocked on the door. A tall, angular
woman opened it. She wore a plain brown dress without decoration.
Her silver hair was drawn into a tight bun and her voice was firm.

"Come in, child. Come in. I heard you were doing a bit of visiting but I thought you might pass along by my door." She glanced at
Napper who stayed quiet.

Judy extended her hand and smiled. "I'm Judy Power. I'm delighted to visit you Mrs. O'Grady. Why would you ever think I'd
pass your house?"

Their hostess led them into a spotless kitchen before she replied. "I believe I make young Darby there a tad uneasy. He's not
sure if I recognised him up in my crab-apple tree earlier the fall."
Napper didn't see the old woman wink as she took Judy's coat. He
looked like a trapped animal. "It was a dark night and I didn't have
my eye-glasses on."

"I'm quite certain, Mrs. O'Grady," Judy said, "that Napper
knows taking anything, including crab-apples, is stealing and he
would never be involved in such a thing."

"You may be right, Miss Power. In any case, it doesn't matter at
Christmas. I heard how you got stranded and couldn't get home."

"Oh, I wouldn't say stranded. John's Pond will be a different place for me to spend Christmas but I know I'll enjoy it."

"Well, you have the right way of thinking. That's good to see in a young woman. Too many girls these days won't do anything for themselves. They just mope around waiting for someone to come along and marry them. "

"That sounds like a good plan if you can make it work. I'd be afraid I'd wait so long that nobody would want me."

"Trust me girl; you won't have that problem. Now, I'm going to put on the kettle and I want you to tell me about yourself."

The old woman prodded the fire with the poker to get it going better and shoved another junk of wood in the stove. She carefully cleaned the wood-dust from the stovetop before filling the kettle with water from a bucket in the porch and placing it on the stove. Then she took Judy's arm and led her to a pair of over-stuffed chairs in the small parlour off the kitchen. The chairs were close enough for each of them to share small tea table. Napper stayed in the kitchen near the parlour entrance while the women got comfortable.

"Now, tell me," Mrs. O'Grady said, "how did a pretty little thing like yourself end up way out here?"

"I came here because I wanted to be a teacher. It's difficult to obtain a position in the city."

"I'm sure you could have found something closer than here."

"Maybe, but I was intrigued when I heard that the people had just built a new school."

"What do you mean?"

"Well, it seemed like a great adventure to go to a place that was so new that it was only just getting its first school. It was like something one would read about in a story of explorers."

"I see," said the old woman. She appeared to be pondering Judy's explanation as she stood up and sauntered into the kitchen. When she reached the stove she looked at Napper.

"Young fellow, I'd like to have a private chat with Miss Power."
She turned to Judy. "Can you give me an hour of your time?"

"Of course," Judy said. "Napper, I can make my own way home
but will you be sure and come over to Mr. and Mrs. Fleming's tomorrow morning? I want to see you."

"All right." He got up to leave.

"Stop there!" Napper froze in his tracks. Maude locked her eyes
on his. "I won't have Miss Power out in the dark by herself. You
come back for her at half past five and I'll have your supper ready.
Mind the time and don't be late."

"Yes ma'am."

"Napper, perhaps it would be a good idea for you to run over to
Mr. and Mrs. Fleming's to let them know where I am."

"OK."

After Napper took his leave Maude O'Grady turned to Judy.
She now had a smile on her face. "I like to keep them a little bit in
dread of me, you know. That way they cause me no trouble."

"I believe you've succeeded. What is it you want to talk to me
about?"

"This will stay between the two of us?"

"Of course, if that's what you want."

"It is." The old woman walked to the window and parted the
curtains with her forefinger to peep outside. It seemed to Judy
that she was checking to be certain they were alone. She let the
curtains close and faced the teacher.

"I've had a good life. My husband, Ben, was a sailor—a bos'un.
He'd be gone for months at a time but he was a good man and
provided well for me."

"That's easy to see," Judy said as she glanced at the quality of
the furniture in the room.

Maude nodded in acknowledgement. "His ship was lost sixteen
years ago on its way from New York. The company said another

ship last saw it off Nantucket. They say it must have wrecked near Sable Island. A lot of ships met their end around there."

"It must be a terrible thing to lose someone you love."

"It's not easy. Ben often said that he knew nothing when he left here but as soon as he started sailing he learned how to read and write. A young fellow who went on to become a captain taught him."

"That's wonderful. I wish I had known him."

"Well, my dear, maybe you can. Maybe you can." Judy was puzzled as Maude leaned forward in her chair and took her by the hand. "Ben sent me letters every chance he got, but…" she lowered her voice to continue, "I can hardly read. I never got the chance to learn much about reading or writing."

Judy bit her lip as she looked into the old woman's eyes. "You mean you don't know what your husband wrote to you?"

"Well, I can read a little bit but I know I'm missing lots of stuff." The old woman leaned closer to the teacher. "Vanity is a terrible thing but I don't want everyone around here to know I can't read and I certainly don't want everyone knowing what's in those letters. I've prayed for someone like you to come along before I died."

"That's not vanity, Mrs. O'Grady; it's dignity. I'm so delighted I came to see you." Judy squeezed the old woman's hands. "Please, get your letters. I'll be honoured to read them for you and I'll read them as often as you want."

Mrs. O'Grady went to her bedroom and brought out a wrapped keepsake box. She passed it to Judy. "Some of these are almost as old as me. We were only courting when he wrote the first ones. I've always been afraid he might have written something, you know, not very proper. I hope he didn't do that."

"Oh, I hope he did! I'll read whatever he wrote." They were laughing as Judy began. "This one is dated September 22nd, 1825—more than sixty years ago—My darling Maude, we made the land at Oporto, Portugal yesterday evening. It was a fine trip across..."

Judy finished four of the letters before a timid knock on the door announced Napper's return. He glanced towards the table as he entered.

"Don't worry, young Darby," Maude said, "I promised you supper and supper you shall have."

"Mrs. O'Grady," Judy said, "it really isn't necessary for you to go to any trouble."

"Trouble? My love, anything that will keep you here with me a few minutes longer is no trouble. I have roast beef ready to be heated up. I baked bread this morning and I have bake-apple jam and fresh cream all ready to go." She tied on her apron as she talked. "Give me five minutes and I'll have the grandest kind of a feast on the table."

A feast it was, and by the time Judy and Napper finally departed both of them were, in Napper's words, 'as full as an egg'. Judy felt happy in a way she never felt before after she promised Mrs. O'Grady that she would be back for another visit in a few days. When they reached the Fleming's house she made Napper promise to come see her tomorrow—Christmas Day.

As Lizzie Fleming took Judy's coat from her Mike said, "You look like the cat that caught the bird. What have you been up to?"

"Mike!" Lizzie said but Judy cut her off.

"He's right, Mrs. Lizzie. I can't hide anything from him. I had a wonderful day—one of the best of my life. This is a lovely Christmas."

Christmas Day was crisp and clear. Judy went to church with the Flemings. Everyone wore their finest and declared 'Merry Christmas' as they shared handshakes, hugs and warm smiles. After church she was thrilled to watch the Flemings unwrap the gifts she gave them. Mike's eyes lit up at the sight of his new porcelain tea mug. Mrs. Lizzie loved the pretty vase Judy arranged to have her mother send from Bowring's on Water Street. The Flemings gave Judy a beautiful knitted sweater and matching scarf.

"You need the right gear if you're going to be riding hand-cats," Mike said as he hugged her.

While they were still admiring each other's gifts young Napper came in through the back door. "Merry Christmas," he said.

"Merry Christmas, young man," Mike said. "Come here. I have something for you." The old man brought out a small box wrapped in red paper. He passed it to Napper. "I thought you might find use for this."

Napper's eyes widened as he took the paper off the box. "It's a pocket knife! Wow! Thanks Mr. Mike. Thanks Mrs. Lizzie!" He opened the blade and ran his finger along the edge.

"Mrs. Lizzie had nothing to do with it, my son. Her present to you is your Christmas dinner, isn't it dear?"

"Uh, ah…why yes, of course. If you will join us."

"Thanks, Mrs. Lizzie."

"You're very welcome, my love," Lizzie said as she kissed him on the forehead while wagging her forefinger at her smiling husband.

"I've always been of the opinion that a pocket knife is the hand-iest tool a man can carry," Mike said. "I figured that if I started you off with something of quality you'd learn to appreciate it and set high standards for yourself."

Mike's words seemed to go over Napper's head as he rubbed his fingers over the knife's polished wood and shining silver trim. "This is the best…."

"I have something for you too," Judy said. She passed Napper a gift wrapped in more red paper.

His smile widened as he tore the paper off. "It's a shirt." He held up the garment for all to see.

"A fine flannel shirt if I'm any judge," Mike said. "I dare say it can handle a frosty day."

"My father mailed it to me to give to you," Judy said. "He says a smart boy needs to dress smart."

"Napper, my darling," Lizzie said as she put her arm around him and squeezed him in a hug, "Miss Power gave you a lovely gift. You can use it until you wear it out."

He nodded, but said nothing. Lizzie squeezed him again and then turned towards the stove and announced that dinner would be ready momentarily. Judy and Mike both noticed her dab the corners of her eyes.

That was the go all Christmas. Judy visited every house in the place and left all of them with an invitation to return. She partook in the songs and dancing at the kitchen parties that sprang up whenever folks came together during the twelve days and through it all she came to know and admire the people she lived among. Oh yes, she made three or four trips back to Maude O'Grady's and read all of those letters over and over again until Maude had them pretty well memorised. On the last night before school reopened she told Mike and Lizzie Fleming that it was the most wonderful Christmas of her life.

TIMES CHANGE

It has been more than a hundred years since Judy Power's Christmas in John's Pond. A lot of people have come and gone since then but folks still talk about her. I expect they always will. We have always hoped that she enjoyed being with us as much as the stories say she did. You see, her being here was one of those things wiser people say was too good to last.

It was the week before Easter. The spring sunshine had released winter's grip on the world. Napper and a handful other young fellows were busy catching pricklies at the low tide. The tiny stickleback minnows came into the harbour in millions every spring for no apparent reason other than to amuse young boys. The lads were soaked to the skin by the time the tide turned to rise making it too hard to nab the little fish. They were standing on the shore trying to figure out what to do next when one of them, Ned Keefe, spotted a sail.

"Look, there's a boat coming in." All eyes turned and squinted at the horizon. Plans for the rest of the day were suddenly clear. "Come on; let's go out on the wharf."

A half-hour later Napper, Ned and their friends were shivering on the wharf as the schooner *Corisande* tied up. Mike Fleming and some other men had seen the ship come in and also waited on the wharf. Mike knew the skipper and greeted him as he came alongside.

"Captain Hughes, it's good to see you. What brings you in here so early in the year?"

"Hello, Mike. We were crossing the bay on our way to St. John's when the bottom fell out of the glass." He gestured to the barometer hanging inside the wheelhouse door. "We're in for hard weather and I'd sooner be in here than out there when it hits."

"Why don't you come over to the house when you get squared away? Lizzie would love to see you again."

"That sounds grand, Mike. I'll take you up on it. Tell Lizzie I'll be there in about an hour's time."

It's strange how one thing leads to so much more. I suppose it's why someone came up with the notion of fate to explain it. Captain Hughes kept his appointment with Mike and Lizzie and, of course, met Judy. When he heard how she missed getting home for Christmas he was kind enough to offer her passage to St. John's so she could spend Easter with her family. She was thrilled to accept. Two days later when the weather was civil again she boarded the schooner for the overnight trip.

No one knows exactly what went wrong; there has been all kinds of speculation. Perhaps the tail end of the storm was still hanging around. The only thing we know for sure is that west of Cape Race the *Corisande* smashed on the rocks.

All hands were lost.

No word of the tragedy reached John's Pond until two days later when Dick Croke went to Whitbourne for the mail. They say that tough old trapper bawled like a baby when he was given the news. It sure knocked the wind out of this place. People figured Mike and Lizzie Fleming would never get over it but they managed. Napper gave them strength.

Mr. Mike and Mrs. Lizzie, along with the mill-owner Mr. Thistle and his wife, went to St. John's for Miss Power's funeral. Dick Croke and Mrs. Maude O'Grady went too. Napper thought it strange how Mrs. Maude turned out to be so nice. After they came back home he went to see Mr. Mike and Mrs. Lizzie just about every day. They talked a lot about Miss Power. He didn't want to let go. Neither did they.

Finally Mike looked at him and said, "Young fellow, we got a big empty house and you're here just about every waking minute; I'm going to talk to your father about letting you come stay with us."

Talking Cec Darby into letting someone else mind one of his youngsters wasn't the hardest job Mike ever tackled. So with no bags and little baggage Napper moved in with the Flemings. You would think such a shift would make him happy but as he explained later in his life that wasn't the case.

"There's no doubt I was better fed and better dressed but that stuff never made me happy or sad. I was already happy enough. I moved in with the Flemings for their sake not mine; they needed someone with them."

A CHRISTMAS LESSON

Napper did something for the Flemings. He put purpose back in their lives. Lizzie had to make sure he had a good breakfast and was dressed warm every day. She had his lunch ready and washed the back of his neck and behind his ears. Mr. Mike made it his business to share the wisdom of his life with the young fellow. He showed Napper all the important things every young man should know. Things like how to snare rabbits, tackle a horse and catch a meal of trout. In between these essentials Mike showed him the fundamentals of carpentry—the same trade, Mike reminded Napper, the good Lord worked at before he got famous.

"I never have to show him anything twice," Mike said to Lizzie one November day when Napper was twelve years old.

"He's the same way with his schoolwork," she said. "He's read every book in the place."

"He's after me to give him a hand to do something special for Christmas this year," Mike said. "He wants to build a nativity crib—one big enough put out in the front yard."

Lizzie laughed. "I never heard tell of anything like that before. Where did he come up with such a notion?"

"I dare say he got it from one of them books he reads. Anyway, he could be doing worse things. "

"Are you going to help him?"

"I suppose. It'll keep me busy too."

Over the next couple of weeks Mike and Napper spent most of their spare time in the shed. The hammering and sawing would go non-stop for a couple of hours and then for the longest time there wouldn't be a sound. Mike explained to Lizzie that was when they were trying to figure out what something looked like over in Bethlehem.

"Can't have the camels looking like humpty-backed horses," he said when she poked her head in around the shed door one snowy evening.

"I suppose not," Lizzie said as she scanned the bits and pieces of shepherds, magi and animals lying around the shed. "Napper, I'm going to take you away from your work for a little while. I need you to run over to the Larkin's for me. I have a pot of stew and a few pans of fresh bread for them."

Mike straightened up from where he was trying to make two boards look like an oriental king. He nodded at Napper.

"You go ahead. They need that bit of supper more than we need to work on this."

"OK," Napper said. He laid his hammer on the bench and hauled on his coat. Lizzie was already making her way to the house. He overtook her with a half-dozen strides and skidded to a stop at the doorstep.

"Wait out here by the door," she said as she went into the porch and took off her snow-boots. "I don't want you bringing snow in through the house." She reappeared a minute later with an iron pot and two loaves of bread wrapped in a cloth. Napper took the food and headed out the lane towards the road. "Mind the pot. It's hot."

"OK."

"Tell Nora she can send back the pot tomorrow."

"OK."

"Hurry now, so they can have it for supper."

"OK."

"I'll have your supper on the table when you get back."

"Don't need it. I got lots here."

"Napper, don't you—" She stopped when she saw him smile, realising he was teasing her. Mike was making his way from the shed. "Why does he get me going like that?"

"Because you make it so easy for him."

She made a motion as if to kick him. "Get inside and wash your hands. I should let the pair of you tend on yourselves. It wouldn't be long before both of you realise how good you have it."

"Ah now my darling, that works both ways. Not many women are lucky enough to have two fine men like us in the house."

She looked to the sky before she closed the door. "I must be a saint."

"You're living with a couple. That's for sure"

Big snowflakes drifted down as Napper walked. The last bit daylight fading to night allowed the glow of kerosene lamps to illuminate the flakes dropping in front of windows. The cosy scene was at odds with Napper's frame of mind. This wasn't the first time he brought food to the Larkin's. Con and Nora Larkin came to John's Pond when the mill was built. They had nothing but they were nice people and worked hard. In a half dozen years they had themselves established with a small house, a stable, some sheep, chickens and five youngsters. Every minute Con was awake he was working in the mill, in the woods or around his house. Nora coaxed carrots, turnips, cabbages and potatoes from a garden behind their house. They were getting by until disaster struck.

Con started cutting his firewood for the winter right after the last log was sawed in the mill. He found a stand of rampikes on the far side of Black Duck pond. Getting to the wood meant crossing a beaver dam on the lower end of the pond. Within a week the weather turned cold and Con took a shortcut across the new ice. He should have known better. Nora raised the alarm when he didn't return home. A search party, Napper among them, spotted the black hole as soon as they got to the pond. They threw in a jigger and snagged Con by the sleeve of his coat. Napper thought about him often—a good man working hard to do his best for his family only to end up in a box. It wasn't fair.

He didn't knock when he reached the Larkin house. He lifted the latch and let himself into the porch and then opened the door to the kitchen. The single lamp was turned down low and he had to peer through the gloom to make out Nora Larkin sitting by the stove. One of her children was in her arms.

"Hello, Nora. Mrs. Lizzie sent over a pot of stew and some fresh bread. I'll lay the pot on the stove to keep it hot." The three oldest children began clamouring for the food before he reached the stove. Nora put the child she had been holding in the chair.

"All of you, get over to the table and leave Napper alone," she said. The children scampered to the chairs around the table. Their mother lifted the cover on the pot and looked inside. "This is wonderful. Tell Mrs. Lizzie I said thanks. "

"I'll tell her," Napper said. He stared at the children waiting for the food. "Is there anything else I can do?"

"Will you stay and have some supper with us?"

"No, Mrs. Lizzie would have a fit. She told me she would have my supper on the table when I get back. She said you can keep the pot until you're finished with it."

"I'll send one of the youngsters around with it tomorrow."

"I'll tell her. Well, I better be going. Me and Mr. Mike are building a Christmas crib." As soon as he uttered the words he wished he had kept quiet.

Neil, the eldest of the children spoke up, "Are you putting up a Christmas tree, Napper?"

"I suppose so."

"I want to cut one, but mom doesn't want me to go in the woods with an axe by myself."

Napper looked at the young fellow and then at his mother. "I'll go with him if you want me to."

"Can we go tomorrow?" Neil asked.

"We don't need a tree," Nora said. She spooned a small dollop of stew onto plates and put one in front of each child. Then she cut three slices of bread in half, giving the children a half slice each. "Oh my, there's plenty here for a couple of days."

"Mom, what about the tree? Will we get one?"

"Eat your supper. Never mind trees." She looked at Napper and lowered her voice. "I don't want them getting too built up about Christmas."

Napper nodded and pulled up the hood on his parka. "See you all later." They were all shouting thanks and good-bye as he made his way outdoors.

In the decades to come Napper Darby spoke often about delivering that pot of stew. He said some things can shape a life. That stew put a turn in his. "We don't need much to get through this world. We want lots but we only need a few things. Hope is one of them. That evening I saw people with no hope and I didn't like the look of it."

"Napper, what's wrong?" Lizzie asked as soon as he came in through the door.

"The Larkins are in bad shape. I thought the youngsters were going to eat me when I went in with the stew. They came after it like dogs."

Lizzie sighed and shook her head. "It's an awful fix to be in—five youngsters and only a bit of government dole coming in. They'd starve if it wasn't for what's being given to them."

"What's going to happen to them? They haven't even got enough kerosene oil to turn up the lamp." He continued to talk while Lizzie laid his supper on the table. "They got nothing for Christmas. She's afraid to get a tree because the youngsters will expect everything to be like other years."

"I don't know what's going to become of them," she said.

"Is there anywhere they can go? Does she have anyone belong to her that can help?"

"Not that I know of. No family came when Con drowned."

Mike Fleming lay on the couch in the corner of the kitchen. He didn't say anything while his wife and Napper were talking. Now he sat up and reached for his pipe and tobacco on the shelf above the couch. Napper turned to him,

"Mr. Mike, do you think anything can be done for them?"

"A great deal, I dare say."

"Like what?"

"Like you eating your supper."

"How's that going to help?"

"Misery loves company. Don't give it any."

"I don't understand…"

"I know you don't. Now, eat your supper and let me have my pipe in peace. Then we'll size up your problem."

A half-hour later all three of them were still sitting at the table. Lizzie poured each of them another cup of tea. Napper's appetite was back and a bun of fresh bread was bearing the brunt of it. He coated each slice with Lizzie's fresh butter and partridgeberry jam but his mind didn't stray far from the Larkins. "There has to be some way to help them."

"What's their problem?" asked Mike.

"They're in the worse kind of shape…"

"Indeed they're not. If they had no house, or no firewood, or if a couple of them were sick it'd be worse."

"Maybe…."

"No maybes. It could be a lot worse."

"But they don't know where their next meal is coming from."

"So what we're talking about is finding a way for them to know they'll always have something to eat. That doesn't look to be the hardest thing in the world to fix. How many homes are here in John's Pond now?"

"About thirty."

"So if every house gave about ten meals a year they'd be in pretty good shape, wouldn't they?"

"Yes, but would everyone do that?"

"I'd say so. Some mightn't be able to do much, but some can do more. It's only one meal every four or five weeks, and don't forget, they can provide some for themselves."

Lizzie looked at Mike. "How would we get it started."

He shook his head and laughed. "It's already started. Sometimes we don't see what's in front of our faces. We've been sending them stuff since Con died; so has just about everyone else."

"True," Lizzie said, "but it's not something she can depend on."

"That's the part needs fixing and now, coming on Christmas, is the right time of the year to fix it."

Napper always chuckled whenever he retold that part of the story later in his life. "That Christmas Mr. Mike Fleming was like a fellow looking to get elected," he said. "Every house he'd go into he be off in a corner having a talk to the man; then he'd take the missus aside and have a word with her. Once he got them going along with him he'd tell the crowd in the next house so they'd want to be part of it too. By the Twelfth Night he had laid out who had to cook and when, who would get firewood, mow the hay and do whatever else had to be done. Nobody had to do much but with all hands working together, we pulled the Larkins through a rough spell."

A FINE CATCH

Napper was fifteen when he finished what schooling was available in John's Pond. He landed a job in the cooper shop at Thistle's mill. In October of the same year Mike Fleming got soaking wet one evening while checking his rabbit snares. That night he had the chills and two days later he was laid up with pneumonia. Mrs. Lizzie tended to him day and night for a week. She applied liniments, poultices and medicines couriered from the doctor in Whitbourne. The prayers of a community were dispatched to heaven but it was all for nothing; she couldn't pull him back. Mike Fleming died on a cold Thursday morning. He stated in his will that Napper was to inherit his house and land on the condition that Lizzie could stay there as long as she was alive.

Napper did well for himself over the next few years. He grew tall and strong, able to keep up with the best men in the mill. Along with his work at the mill, he was always able to make an extra dollar with the carpenter's tools and skills that Mike left him. It was enough to keep any man busy; he scarcely noticed the years slip by.

One Saturday morning in August of his twenty-second year Napper woke and realised that he had a rare day with no work scheduled.

"Mrs. Lizzie," he announced as he came downstairs for break-fast, "I'm going to dig a few worms and go in to Billy-Boy pond for the day."

"That sounds wonderful," she said. "I'd love a meal of trout. I'll pack a lunch for you."

"Thanks. Some bread and jam will be enough and some tea. I'll make a fire and boil the kettle when I get hungry."

An hour later he was ambling along Whitbourne road with his trouting pole in his hand and his lunch bag on his back. The morning sun was already warm on his face and the air was thick with the fragrance of lupines. Bumblebees buzzed around the roadside flowers and dragonflies dipped and darted about hunting for flies. He took his time and enjoyed the walk. About three miles in he came to the point where he had to leave the road and take the short path across a marsh to the pond. He had only taken a few steps on the path when he was startled by a calling voice.

"Hello! Excuse me, sir! Can you help me?"

He scanned the area and spotted the source of the voice. "What the...?" He stared at the figure walking towards him and then yelled, "Stay there! I'm coming!" He dropped his trouting pole and trotted towards the stranger, trying to figure out what anyone was doing in the middle of nowhere so early in the day. "What, what are you...?"

"*What* am I? Have you never seen a lady before?"

"No...I mean yes, but not...I'm sorry. I meant to say...ah...not three miles in the woods."

"It's more like ten miles."

"...Well yes, I suppose. It depends on which way you're going. Who...ah...who..."

"Are you trying to ask my name?"

"Napper. I'm Napper Darby and I was going trouting, over there, and, and …do you need something?" Napper's mouth dried up and his tongue wouldn't work right. She was about his age and even there, on the red clay road, she radiated in the August sunshine. Her blue eyes matched her dress and the summer sky above them. Her blonde hair sat above the prettiest face he had ever seen. A faint scent of perfume teased him and made him want to get closer. Her voice was cultured and musical. She extended her hand to Napper, who needed a second before he realised he was supposed to shake it. Her smile completed the easy task of taking control of him.

"I'm pleased to meet you. Napper Darby. I'm Bertha Curtis, and yes, I do need something. I need help with my horse."

"What horse?"

"I left him a little bit in the road. He won't go for me."

"What's wrong with him?"

"I don't know. He won't move."

"Let's go see." They started in the road. "Is he hurt?"

"I don't think so. The man who rented him to me said he was a fine horse."

"Rented him? From who?"

"A man in Whitbourne. I came in on the train yesterday evening. I planned to stay there last night but it was such a nice evening I decided instead to try to get a ride to John's Pond. The man to whom I was recommended wasn't feeling up to the trip but offered me the use of his horse and wagon for fifty cents."

"You mean you've been on the road all night?"

"I'm afraid the horse was rather slow and I just couldn't bring myself to whip him."

"So you were in the woods by yourself, all night? Weren't you afraid?"

"Afraid? Why? Because I'm a woman?"

"No, that's not what I meant. I mean lots of people, lots of men, won't travel by themselves at night."

"Is there anything in here to be afraid of?"

"Well, no…"

"Then why should I be afraid? Well, to be honest, I was a little bit apprehensive at first but when I realised how peaceful it was I enjoyed it."

"You're quite a woman." The words were out before he realised what he was saying. His face turned scarlet as her eyes locked on his. He was about to try to explain himself when she lit up the world around them with another smile.

"Thank you. That's a very kind thing to say."

She did most of the talking as they walked; for the first time in his life he found words hard to come by. She was the new teacher and she was from St. John's. He answered her questions about John's Pond and did his best not to look stupid, but it was hard to concentrate. Reality came charging back, however, when they crested a small hill and he caught sight of her horse.

"Good lord, that's Ted."

"Ted? Who's Ted?" she asked.

"That thing is the oldest horse in Whitbourne—probably the oldest horse in the country. No wonder you were on the road all night."

"He was surprisingly slow."

"I'm surprised he lived to make it this far."

"Perhaps the man should not have rented him to me?"

"The sleeveen that owns him would rent his own soul for the price of a drink."

"What shall I do?"

"Well, it's no good trying to get him to John's Pond. He'll probably drop dead in the traces. We'll turn him loose to find his way home and I'll get my horse to haul the wagon the rest of the way."

"Should I go with you?"

"You can if you like but it's about three miles. I can be there and back in less time than it will take you to walk there in that outfit and you said you're not afraid."

"I did say that, didn't I?" His heart raced as she smiled again.

Napper took the harness off Ted and threw it in the wagon. He pointed the horse on the road to home and slapped him on the rump. Ted plodded away.

"He'll be OK if he doesn't get lost; he's pretty much blind too." He passed his lunch bag to her. "Help yourself to whatever is in it; Mrs. Lizzie usually tucks in a little treat for me. I won't be long. There's nothing around here to bother you except the flies."

She hit him again with her smile, leaving his legs wobbly and his mouth all but useless. "I think I shall be quite comfortable here while I await your return." She was still smiling as he began his jog to John's Pond. His reactions to her had not gone unnoticed.

Napper returned in less than half the time that Bertha expected him to be gone. In a few minutes he had his horse, a lively red mare named Nell, hitched to the wagon and they were underway at a brisk trot.

"Where are you staying?"

"I don't have a place yet but an acquaintance of mine told me there is a lady who keeps boarders. Do you know her?"

"That'd be Mrs. Carey, Carey's Hotel, but she mostly keeps men working in the mill." Bertha frowned. He laughed. "Don't worry. We'll find you a good place. We'll stop at our house and get something figured out."

Minutes later they passed the first homes in John's Pond. Napper grinned when he saw the faces of the people they passed. He leaned to Bertha and said, "I have to stay away from everyone for the next few hours."

"Why?"

"To drive them nuts while they try to figure out who you are." Both of them were laughing most of the way to Napper's house where Mrs. Lizzie was delighted to welcome the young woman.

"My, oh my. I was only expecting Napper to bring back a few trout. He outdid himself this time for sure."

"What you catch depends on how good the bait is," Napper said before Bertha could speak. It didn't work out the way he expected. The young teacher laid down the valise she was holding and walked to Napper until her face was only inches from his.

"Tell me sir, do I look like a fish? Are you a worm?"

"I didn't mean anything…I'm sorry…I—"

Bertha turned to Mrs. Lizzie and broke into a big smile, "Isn't it sweet when they get like this?"

Mrs. Lizzie laughed out loud and looked at Napper, "You'll have to figure out who's the bait and who's the fish." Turning to Bertha she said, "I can see I'm going to like you. Come in, my love, and we'll have a cup of tea."

Napper knew it wasn't the sun burning his face as he followed them into the house.

THE CHRISTMAS PLAY

Bertha Curtis took a room with Will and Mae Kerrivan and began teaching in John's Pond. She was liked and respected by her students and by the other residents of the village. Napper didn't often have any reason to be in her company but when they did meet she always took a moment to chat with him—something Ned Keefe pointed out as he and Napper walked home from the mill on an evening in October.

"She won't give any other fellow in this place the time of day," Ned said, "but she'll stop and wear the ears off you."

"Don't be so foolish. She hardly says much more than hello."

"She says more to you than she does to all the rest of us put together and you're a fool if you don't make something of it."

"The only reason she talks to me is because I helped her that day she was trying to get here."

"It makes no difference. You should be making the most of it. You're not going to see many like her around here."

Napper didn't need Ned to tell him that he wouldn't get many opportunities to court a woman like Bertha Curtis. His problem was that he had no idea how to even get started. Years later Bertha said that his bewilderment was so obvious that she took it upon herself to do something about it. Napper was in his shed one morning in early December building shelves for Thistle's store when a boy stuck his head in around the door. He gave Napper a note and said that he had been told to wait for an answer. Napper unfolded the paper.

> *Mr. Darby,*
>
> *I'm planning to have the children perform The Christmas Story this month, however we require some help from a carpenter. Would you be able to assist us? If you can, please come to the school after classes this evening. Please send your answer with this messenger. Thank you.*
> *Miss Curtis*

"Tell her I'll be there."

Napper arrived at the school, with his toolbox, three o'clock that evening. It was already decorated with wreaths of fragrant fir boughs and paper snowflakes. A Christmas tree stood in the corner. The teacher was helping several students rehearse their lines. More students waited for her attention. Napper noticed how she was in control of everything happening around her. She greeted him.

"Mr. Darby, thank you for coming. I am in dire need of assistance." She smiled the same way that Napper remembered from their meeting on the road. This time he smiled back.

"Happy to help. What do you need done?"

"As you know, we're planning to perform, 'The Christmas Story'. We've managed to make costumes and most of the other things but we still need a manger."

"That shouldn't be a problem. How big do you want it?"

About an hour later Napper had the manger built to the teacher's specifications. He accepted Bertha's invitation to watch the students put it to use in the final practice of the evening.

"Thank you everybody," she said as the practice ended. "It still needs work, but it's getting better every time we do it. I also want to thank Mr. Darby for his kind assistance today." Napper blushed as the children clapped for him. "Now, everybody go home, do your chores and make sure you do your homework." In seconds the classroom was empty.

"It didn't take them long to bail out," he said as he pulled on his own coat.

"It's getting late and they're hungry. I really appreciate you coming here to help today. It makes my work so much easier." She smiled and stood close enough for him to catch the scent that he remembered from the first time they met.

"Any time. Just let me know." He was smiling too. Neither of them moved.

"Thank you. I'll keep that in mind." She kept her eyes on his.

"I...ah, I wanted to speak to you anyway," he said.

"Oh? About what?"

His mouth was dry. "I wanted to ask you...well, there's going to be a dance here before Christmas...after the concert...and I, if it's OK with you, I was wondering if—"

"Are you offering to escort me to the dance?"

"If you don't mind, unless you're going with someone else—"

She smiled. His legs were shaking. "There isn't anybody else. I would be honoured to go with you. Thank you for asking me."

"Anytime, just...I mean, thank you."

She looked out the window. "Oh my, the evenings are closing in so fast. I hate walking home in the dark."

"I'll go with you if you like."

"What about your tool box?"

"I can lay it outside and get it on my way back."

"I don't want to put you to any more trouble."

"It's no trouble. Really."

"Thank you. Let me get my coat." Moments later Napper secured the school door and they were making their way along the road. A dusting of snow lay on the frozen ground. "I don't want to slip and fall," she said as she linked her arm into his.

There's no doubt but a strapping young man like Napper Darby could have covered the ground between the school and Will Kerrivan's house a lot quicker than he did that evening. He could have done it in half or maybe even quarter of the time he took. You would not have needed a particularly keen eye to see that she could have been walking faster too. Even so, they arrived at their destination sooner than either of them wanted. Of course, neither of them said that to the other; it wouldn't be proper.

"Are you coming in?" she asked when they reached the Kerrivan's door.

"I'll stop in for a minute and say hello to Will and Mae."

As they went inside, Mae Kerrivan opened the kitchen door to allow light from the lamp to brighten the porch. "Oh, hello Napper. I wasn't expecting to see you."

"Hello, Mae. It was dark and I…"

"Napper helped us make some things for the play and then was kind enough to accompany me so I wouldn't have to walk home in the dark."

"That was nice of you, Napper," Mae said. "Stop in and have some supper."

"No, thanks. I'd love to but Mrs. Lizzie will have my supper on the table."

"Who's that, Mae?" a man's voice asked from inside the kitchen.

Napper answered first. "Hello, Will. It's me, Napper."

Mae and Bertha moved into the kitchen. Will came to the porch door where he could see Napper. "Come in and have a cup of tea to warm yourself."

"Thanks, but some other time."

"What brings you out here on a frosty evening like this?" Will asked, a grin on his face.

"He wanted to make sure I got home safe and sound," Bertha said.

"I dare say he did," Will said, his grin widening.

"Now, you mind yourself," his wife cut in. "Leave Napper alone. It's not your concern."

Napper could feel his face warming and was happy to be in the shadows of the porch. Bertha was smiling and her face was flushed too, but there was no way of knowing whether it was the winter chill or Will's jibes causing the crimson.

"I can't stay," Napper said. "Mrs. Lizzie will have my supper on the table and she'll be worried if I'm late." He made a quick exit before Will could get in any more wisecracks. He felt strange on the walk home, happy but nervous. Did Bertha really like him or was she just amusing herself with him? She seemed to be sincere and she was going to the dance with him; but why him? She could have her pick of any men she met. He could think about little else as he lay awake in his bed that night and stared at the ceiling illuminated by the reflection of the full moon on the snow.

Not far away Bertha Curtis snuggled under her quilts. Her mind was racing. She took a liking to Will and Mae Kerrivan as soon as she moved in with them back in August. Mae doted on her, now that her own eight children were raised and out in the world. Will was a foreman in the mill, in his own house and everywhere in between. He was a bald-headed, barrel-chested giant who never seemed to be still. His voice, accustomed to being heard over the din of mill-saws, stayed at the same volume all the time. At first glance it was hard to imagine the sophisticated young woman from the city having anything to do with him but she took to him like a duck to water. Today experts would offer profound explanations for her affection to the Kerrivans, especially her attachment to Will, but there really wasn't much to it. The simple fact is that they were the first real family she ever knew.

Her right hand clutched a book tight to her breast as she stared at the ceiling above her bed. Was this was the place she was meant to be? It was hard to know considering the twists and turns in her life up to this point. Was she meant for something better? She could have ended up in so many other places—so many worse places.

BERTHA'S STORY

"It's too late for bawling now. You should have thought about this before you latched on to some sailor you'd never see again." The girl on the bed writhed in agony. It was her second full day in labour. The midwife assigned to her by the matron of St. Bridgid's home for unwed mothers took smug satisfaction from the girl's torment. "You won't be so loose with yourself when you leave here will you?"

"Please…help me…I can't go on…please…oh, God…"

"You have no choice but go on. It's too late to go back. Remember this the next time you want to have a fling for yourself."

It continued for another ten hours—the physical agony and the pious torment of the midwife—until finally, thirty-five hours after her labour started, the girl pushed a child into the world. The young mother knew her time with her baby would be short.

"Please, pass it here. Let me hold it. What is it?"

"A girl. She looks like she's all there. Please God she'll turn out better than her mother. Here, get used to holding her." The midwife wrapped the baby in a thin blanket and passed her to her mother. Anything the young mother said to the child went un-heard by the midwife. It was only when she turned to tell the girl to stop the new-born's crying that she saw something was amiss. The mother's eyes were closed, her baby cradled in her dead arms.

An undertaker was summoned to tend to the mother. The mid-wife had her dinner and moved on to her next patient. A scullery maid was given a break from her drudgery in the kitchen to carry the baby girl to St. Anne's orphanage.

Fourteen years later the girl was lost in her thoughts as she swept the orphanage floor. It was two days before Christmas, 1897.

"Bertha, come here. I want to speak with you." A nun waited for the girl's attention.

Startled, the girl stood the broom against the wall and pre-sented herself in front of the nun. "Sister?"

"You continue to apply yourself to your studies," the nun said.

"Yes, Sister." The girl's frock hung shapeless and loose. A blue ribbon tied her blonde hair in a ponytail. Her face was pretty, but thin. Her blue eyes appeared large, maybe because the rest of her body was gaunt, maybe due to wariness. She knew from experi-ence that she had little control over her life in St. Anne's.

"I have a nice surprise for you."

"Sister?" Her wariness increased.

"You know that some of our wealthy benefactors often invite orphans to spend Christmas with them. This year Mr. and Mrs. William Kent have offered to take one of you into their home. We have decided that it should be you." The girl allowed a small smile, but still hesitated, expecting some price to be asked. The nun saw her anxiety. "You're going to have a fine Christmas. The Kents will treat you just like one of their own. Come now, we have to get you ready."

Two hours later she was bathed, coached on her manners and standing inside the front entrance of St. Anne's awaiting the Kent's carriage. She carried a small bag that held a change of underclothes, a borrowed dress and little else. At the appointed time a pair of handsome black horses, trotting in unison, pulled a carriage to the front door. The coachman stopped the horses and then jumped down from his seat to open the carriage door for her. The horses snorted and shook their bridles. She got the feeling they were annoyed at this unusual stop and were anxious to get moving again. She could feel the eyes of her fellow orphans watching her, envious of her good fortune, not knowing that at that moment she would change places with any of them.

"Hello," a voice boomed as she climbed into the carriage. "So you're the girl who will be spending Christmas with us. What's your name?" The speaker wore a top hat and a black wool overcoat—expensive clothes on a man who looked comfortable in the expensive carriage.

"Bertha, sir. Bertha Curtis." She wasn't expecting anybody else to be riding with her. An older man, from a similar station in life judging by the cut of his cloth, occupied the seat opposite. The older man moved over to give her room to sit.

"I'm Mr. Kent and this is Mr. Mullock," Mr. Kent said, pointing to the older gentleman.

Mr. Mullock nodded but said nothing. His silver hair and beard were trimmed short so that Bertha could see the line of his jawbone. His black top hat, the kind fashionable among the powerful, cast a shadow over his face. His dark eyes peered at her from under the hat.

"It's a pleasure to meet you, sir," she said. Another nod was the only reply. The carriage exited the orphanage grounds and made its way east towards Circular Road. Bertha watched people bustling along the sidewalk. They were bundled against the December cold. She shivered. Mr. Kent noticed it. He shifted to one end of his carriage seat and then flipped up the other half to reveal a storage space underneath from out of which he pulled a comforter.

"Stand up," he said. She stood, giving him room to spread the comforter over her seat. He motioned for her to sit again and wrapped the comforter around her. Immediately she felt the warmth. "How's that? Any better?"

"Yes. Thank you, sir." She looked at him and smiled. He smiled back.

"Always treat a guest the best you can I say or don't invite them at all."

Ten minutes later the carriage turned off Circular Road and into a cobblestone driveway. It seemed to take forever to reach the end of the driveway and come to a stop. Bertha peered out the window to see the widest steps she had ever seen. The steps led up to a set of doors that looked bigger than the ones in the Cathedral of St. John the Baptist. Statues of men on horses, only bigger than real men and real horses, stood on each side of the doors. Light flowed from the windows alongside of the doors and from the windows above the doors and from the windows above those windows. Young Bertha could easily believe she had been summoned to a royal palace.

"Well, here we are," Mr. Kent said. "What do you think?"

"It's beautiful," she said, as she stared up and down and all around, trying to take it all in. Mr. Mullock said nothing as he led the way inside.

Bertha followed them through the colossal doors and stopped breathing. This, she was later to learn, was the great hall. Four chandeliers beamed light from high above. The polished furniture offered a rich, warm radiance of its own. A bonfire roaring in a massive fireplace toasted the room with warmth she never knew existed in winter. But it was the colours that stopped her. She was rocked at the sight of colours that she couldn't have imagined— brilliant red carpets, royal blue drapes and emerald green upholstery. The colours announced that this was a world far different from the grey one she knew.

"We're home," called Mr. Kent as they shut the door. A maid appeared to take their coats. She tended to Bertha with the same efficiency that she showed to the gentlemen.

"Thank you, Mary," Mr. Mullock said as she took the garments.

"Dinner is ready to be served now if it is convenient," said the maid.

"In about five minutes," Mr. Kent said. "I'm starved but we need to do some introductions first. Would you ask my wife and daughters to join us?"

"Right away, sir," the maid said, and was gone.

"Ah, you have her," a woman said as she swept in from an adjoining room and saw the girl. Bertha figured the woman had seen both sides of forty, but not much more. Her dress was plain but well cut and not cheap. Her brown hair was carefully coiffured—as was her smile, Bertha thought.

"We do indeed," her husband said, "and as soon as Charlotte and Kathleen join us I will have the pleasure of introducing her."

"We're here father." Two young women entered through the same door as their mother. They appeared not to see Bertha as each of them kissed their father and grandfather on the cheek. They were about least seventeen or eighteen years old and, Bertha could see, enjoyed the latest fashions. Everything about them, from their curled hair to their slippered feet, spoke of wealth and luxury. Bertha would be happy if they never saw her but that was not to be.

"My dears, I would like you to meet Miss Bertha Curtis, our Christmas guest. Bertha, this is my wife, Mrs. Kent, and our daughters, Charlotte and Kathleen. Of course, you have already met my wife's father, Mr. Mullock. Ladies, please welcome Bertha to our home."

Mrs. Kent stepped forward first and extended her hand. "Welcome, Bertha. I want you to feel right at home here. If you need anything at all Mary or any of the other servants will help you."

"Hello Bertha, I'm Charlotte." The older of the two offered her hand. "It's such a delight to be able to share Christmas with the less fortunate. I hope you enjoy your stay with us."

"I'm Kathleen," the other girl said. She smiled and continued to hold Bertha's hand as she spoke, but Bertha felt no warmth from the hand or from her words. "I really want you to have fun while you're here. I know we're all older than you, but maybe we can have a chat after dinner?"

"OK," the orphan replied. Her years in the orphanage had sharpened her wits when it came to protecting herself and, although they said nothing wrong, she sensed no welcome in their words.

"Ah yes, dinner," Mr. Kent said. "Let's get to it. I'm starved." He led them from the great room and into the dining room where the table was set for six. The table was wider, taller and almost as long as the ones she was familiar with—the ones that seated twenty orphans at a time. The chairs were the biggest and heaviest she had ever seen. She struggled to drag one close enough to the table to be able to eat without standing

Mr. Mullock said grace as soon as they were seated. Mary appeared with a tureen of beef and vegetable soup. Bertha was delighted and surprised. She liked soup and this was delicious but she never expected rich people to eat the same kind of meals to which she was accustomed. The difference between rich people and orphans became apparent after the soup was finished. Nobody got up from the table to do the dishes. Instead, they all sat there while Mary served roast beef with Yorkshire pudding. Cake and custard followed while a pitcher of lemonade waited in front of her to wash it all down. Any part of it would have been a royal treat for the young girl; altogether, it was a feast from her dreams.

Bertha spent all Christmas with the Kents but the parts she always talked about, indeed the only parts she seemed to remember, were the evening of her arrival and two events from Christmas day—a Christmas day unlike any other in her young life. She didn't wake until after eight o'clock, something that would never happen among the cheer-starved waifs at St. Anne's. She lay in bed for a few minutes trying to hear some movement in the house. Finally, she got out of bed, crept to the bedroom door and opened it a few inches. Voices could be heard downstairs so she tiptoed down the steps and stood outside the parlour door. She could hardly believe her eyes and ears.

A mountain of gifts surrounded Charlotte and Kathleen. Festive wrapping lay from one end of the room to the other. Over and under the paper Bertha could see hats still in hatboxes, silk scarves, coats cut from the best cloth and trimmed with prime fur. There were dresses in a rainbow of colours lying on the armchairs and sofas. Shoes, slippers, boots and stockings hung from packages. But not only clothing, there was jewellery and cosmetics, board games and sheet music; in short, the room held every amusement a young woman could imagine. But as her eyes came to grips with the sight before them it was young Bertha's ears that delivered the greatest surprise.

"I'm certain this hat came in to Bowering's two months ago," Charlotte said. "They will be the most common around the city this year. *I won't* be seen in one."

Kathleen wrinkled her nose as she held up one of the most exquisite dresses Bertha had ever seen. "Mother, *you know* Evelyn Squires wore this identical dress at the Commercial Society ball just three weeks ago. I can't wear it."

"I'm sorry, dear," Mrs. Kent said. "We can pass that on to someone else and get you a better one." Kathleen did not reply. Instead she glanced at a gleaming leather boot, lifted it with her foot and flicked it aside as she examined a coat trimmed with shimmering mink fur.

"This is nice," she said. Her mother smiled.

"I wouldn't wear it to church today," Charlotte said. "Angela Meyers will probably be wearing one just like it. Her father was in London at the same time as father. They may have made the same purchases."

"I have no idea what Mr. Meyers did in London," her father said. His tone sounded severe for a man able to do so much for his family. "It's a big city. We just happened to be in the same hotel."

"Maybe, but I won't take any chances," Kathleen said. "I'll know if anyone else has one like it by New Year's Day. If no one does, I'll wear it to the governor's New Year's levee."

Bertha went unnoticed for more than five minutes while Charlotte and Kathleen examined their gifts and found fault to some extent with most of them. She was thinking about retreating to her bedroom, leaving the Kents unaware that she had witnessed their Yuletide afflictions, when a hand on her shoulder startled her.

"Good morning young woman and Merry Christmas." It was Mr. Mullock. He was dressed in a fine white shirt and collar. A silver watch fob crossed his waistcoat and he smelled of a delightful aftershave.

"Merry Christmas to you, sir," she said. She was surprised to see a small smile cross his face.

"Let's go in and see if Father Christmas has remembered you and I." He guided her into the parlour. "Happy Christmas, everyone."

Charlotte and Kathleen ran to hug him right away. "Merry Christmas, Grand-dad." They looked at him with anticipation.

"Let me see. Let me see. I'm sure I have something for you." He made a great show of searching his pockets and pausing as if trying to remember while Charlotte and Kathleen, knowing the happy routine from years past, bounced and squealed in delight. "I remember now...no, that's not right...that's what I was going to get but I changed my mind...let me think...oh yes, now I remember."

He looked at a china cabinet on the far wall and made a motion to step towards it. The girls raced him to it. They opened the doors and pulled out the drawers, searching for something unfamiliar.

"There's nothing here. I can't find anything. Where is it?"

They turned to see him standing by the bookcase on the opposite wall. He took a book from the top shelf allowing him to reach behind the other books and retrieve two small packages. He smiled as he passed one to each granddaughter.

They tore the wrappings off and opened the cases inside. Each held a set of decorative combs fashioned from silver, gold, mother of pearl and ivory.

"There are no others like them in this city," he said, "or any other city for that matter. I ordered them two years ago when I was in New York. I planned to give them to you last year but they weren't ready in time; the finest jeweller on Fifth Avenue won't be rushed."

"Thank you, Grand-dad! Thank you!" Bertha watched both of them peck him on the cheek and allow him to hug them. Moments later the gifts so thoughtfully chosen were left on the parlour table. Mr. Mullock may not have noticed because he had turned his attention to Bertha.

"Now my little one, come here. I haven't forgotten you." From behind a chair he pulled a large, flat package and passed it to her. "Go ahead and open it."

She was shaking as she tugged on the wrappings, trying not to damage the pretty paper. Soon, she succeeded in uncovering the box and lifted the cover. Inside was a coat—a coat she would never have dreamed of owning. It was made from fine Merino wool, dyed deep emerald green, soft to touch and trimmed with black fox fur. Two rows of black-glass buttons covered with a gold lustre marched its entire length and adorned the pockets. Its shape, its colour, its smell, everything about it exuded affluence. She didn't lift it from the box, instead her hands raced across it from the collar to the hem and up to the pockets. Then, without warning, sobs wracked her body. She couldn't stop them, nor could she stop herself from running to Mr. Mullock and throwing her arms around the old man. She buried her face in his waistcoat and clung to him while her sobs grew more intense.

"There, there, my little one," he said as he stoked the back of her head. "It's only a coat, just a little coat."

"It's beautiful. Thank you. Thank you." She squeezed him harder.

"I'm delighted that you think so much of it," he said as he finally pried himself from her grasp. Her gave her a handkerchief to dry her eyes and blow her nose. "I will wager, however, that it will look much better on you than it does in the box. Allow me, if you will…" He took the coat from the box and held it for her to put on. He then steered her to a mirror where she stood speechless, her gaze alternating from the vision in the glass to the approving face of her benefactor. She might have stayed there for the next twelve days if Mr. Kent hadn't spoken up.

"I hope it won't cause you too much excitement but we also have a little something for you." Mrs. Kent left her husband's side to take Bertha by the hand and direct her to the only box in the room with its wrapping undisturbed. Bertha was more composed as she opened this gift. Still, there was no mistaking her joy upon seeing its contents. A dress, sewn from deep burgundy satin, greeted her eyes. But there was more—underneath the dress Bertha found a bonanza—blouses, stockings, shoes, a hat and gloves, all new and her size. There was a box of pencils, writing paper, perfumed soap and even a huge box of chocolate fudge. Any single item would have been a treasure for her; altogether it left her numb.

"Thank you, thank you all so much." She hugged Mr. and Mrs. Kent and, without hesitating, she hugged Charlotte and Kathleen. Then she sought out Mr. Mullock and hugged him again. She was still clinging to him when Mrs. Kent spoke to him.

"Father, I have a little something I think you will like." She passed a small package to her father. He sat in an armchair to unwrap it. Bertha stood beside him.

"*Captain's Courageous,* Kipling's new book. I've been meaning to buy it." It was a leather-bound edition—a beautiful book written, Bertha knew, by a famous author. The smell of the new leather binding mingled with the scent of his aftershave and the aroma from his pipe tobacco.

"It's beautiful," she said.

He looked up at her. "It is, isn't it? Do you like to read?"

"I read every chance I get. I've read just about everything in St. Anne's."

"Really? How would you like to help me read this?"

"How can I help you to read?"

"Well, I have two problems with reading these days. My eyes are not as sharp as they once were and I tend to fall asleep. Now, if you were to read to me for an hour or two each night we would get through this fine book in no time. What do you say?"

"I'd love to. When will we start?"

"How about when things settle down later on this afternoon? In the meantime let's have some breakfast and then you can show off those new clothes on the way to the church."

That day brought a great turn to Bertha's life. It didn't occur during tumult of the morning. It came with no more fanfare than is given to a helmsman putting an ocean liner on new course. In fact, like the passengers on a liner, she never knew it took place. It was about four in the afternoon when she asked Mr. Mullock if he would like to start reading. He agreed, adding that he was feeling the effects of the food and drink, and she had better keep an eye on him to be sure he stayed awake or she might have to repeat her reading. They settled into armchairs in the parlour and she opened the book. He was surprised to feel no desire to sleep as she read. The story was captivating. Her voice was clear and pleasant. The old man noted that she did not hesitate or stumble over words. He saw that she was enjoying the book as much as him.

She read for about an hour before the evening meal was served. After the meal he carried his coffee into the parlour again only to discover her already there engrossed in the book.

"Going ahead without me, are you?" he said.

"Oh, I'll read it all to you. It's really good." She turned back to the page where they left off.

"No, no, that's fine. We'll pick it up again tomorrow. You're quite a good reader."

"Thank you, sir"

"And you have good manners." He held up his hand to stop her before she could reply. "Tell me, what do you plan to do with yourself?"

"I don't know. I'd love to travel around the world but I suppose I will have to marry someone like you to do that." She smiled as laughter came from the bottom of his belly. "I think, if I could, I'd like to be a teacher."

"That's a noble profession for a young woman. I'm sure you will be successful if you really want to do it."

Later that evening a parade of distinguished guests came to the Kent residence. They were the businessmen, lawyers and doctors of the city. Bertha saw that they regarded Mr. Mullock as an important man. All of the visitors went out of their way to shake his hand and extend the compliments of the season to him. He in turn included Bertha in his introductions not as an orphan but as a family friend. She noticed that after the introductions Mr. Mullock spent an unusually long time with one of them, a Mr. Laymen. It was strange that she should remember the man for it was almost three years later before she saw him again.

The Christmas she spent with the Kent's was a memory stashed in the back of Bertha's mind as she approached her seventeenth birthday in the spring of 1900. A new century was upon the world—a century that some predicted might see even more changes than the last one, if that was possible. Bertha's concerns were more immediate. It was time for her to leave St. Anne's and she had no idea where she would go.

Nobody had told her to get out but she knew the way of the place and if she wasn't gone by the fall the matter would be forced. Not that she disagreed with the need for her to leave. St. Anne's could barely provide the necessities of life for the children; housing young adults was out of the question. She had few options. Most of the shops and stores employed a few women and she already made enquiries at some of the better ones but received no offers. That left going 'in service' as a maid for some well-to-do family. It would provide a roof and meals and drudgery for the rest of her life. Of course, she might marry a fine man but fine men don't marry maids. The matter rarely left her mind and she was pondering it one morning as she took her turn drying the breakfast dishes. Alice, the cook, came in carrying some packages. She was taking off her coat when she noticed Bertha in the kitchen and spoke to her.

"Didn't the Kents take you in for Christmas a few years ago?"

"Three years ago, why?"

"Did you meet old man Mullock?"

"I did. He was a wonderful man."

"Well, I'm afraid you won't be seeing him anymore. I just came from the butcher shop and they were saying that he died last night."

"Oh, my. He was a nice man—the nicest one of all of them."

"That's what the butchers were saying too. You should think about going to his funeral."

Bertha hesitated only a second before replying. "Yes, yes, I'll definitely go. He went out of his way to be nice to me. It's the least I can do."

It was three days after Mr. Mullock's funeral when Bertha was summoned to the matron's office. Her stomach was in a knot as she approached the door. She expected that this was the meeting she had been dreading. St. Anne's, even with its privations, was the only home she knew. The notion of leaving terrified her. Her knock on the matron's door was barely loud enough to be heard.

"Come in." The matron smiled as Bertha entered. "Bertha, an acquaintance of yours has come to see you." A well-dressed gentleman sat in one of the two chairs in front of the matron's desk.

"I'm sorry, an acquaintance?" The sight of the man brought confusion and relief. She had a reprieve.

"Yes. Mr. Layman hoped that you might remember him."

"Mr. Layman?" He had her attention now. "Oh yes, of course I remember you, from the Kent's. You were a friend of Mr. Mullock." She extended her hand to the gentleman who stood to accept it.

"It's so nice to see you again, Miss Curtis. I hardly recognised you at the funeral. You've grown to a lovely young woman."

"Why…uh…thank you, sir."

He smiled and indicated that she should sit in the vacant chair next to him. He waited for her to be seated before he took his own chair again. "Miss Curtis, I have come here today for reasons of duty."

"Sir?"

"As you have stated, I was indeed Mr. Mullock's friend and his closest confidante. I was also his solicitor and it is in that capacity that I am here." Seeing the confusion on Bertha's face, he continued. "You knew Mr. Mullock as a well-to-do man?"

"He looked like a millionaire to me."

"Actually he was that several times over and was for most of his long life but not all of it. There was a time when he owned less than you."

"I don't have anything."

"You have a roof over your head, an education and you know many people in this city. He had none of those things when he was your age. He once told me that when he got off the ship from Ireland the only thing he owned was a belly with plenty of spare room."

"How did he get so rich?"

"He worked hard and smart. He was honest so people trusted him and did business with him but he always said that the thing that served him best was that he was a good judge of people."

"What do you mean?"

"He always seemed to know who he could trust to do business with and who he should avoid. He said it was something he learned when he couldn't afford to make mistakes. He pegged you to be one he could depend on."

"I'm afraid I still don't understand."

"You made a deep impression on him. He saw much of himself in you—how you valued the good things you were given, how you had worked hard to be able to read so well, your good manners. As soon as I walked into his house that Christmas he pointed you out to me and told me that he wanted to make provisions for you."

"Provisions?"

"Yes. Since that time he has included an extra contribution in his annual gift to this orphanage to ensure that you would have a place to live. He intended to approach you soon regarding your future. Sadly, that cannot happen now but he did take precautions, on my advice I should add, to ensure your well-being. You have been named a beneficiary in his will. Mr. Mullock was a strong believer in giving a helping hand to people who are willing to help themselves. I believe you told him that you wanted to become a teacher. Is that still the case?"

"Why, yes…but it was only a dream…"

"That is no longer the case. Mr. Mullock has bequeathed sufficient funds to pay for your tuition, books, board and lodging, and provide a small allowance for your personal needs while you attend St. Bride's Teachers College at Littledale."

"Oh my, oh…Are you sure? Why would he do something like that for me?"

"Because, as I said, he was a tremendous judge of character and knew in whom he should put his confidence. He also left you a personal memento and instructed me to deliver it." The lawyer reached into his satchel and took out a book. He handed it to Bertha. It was the volume of *Captains Courageous* that she had read to Mr. Mullock. Her hands shook as she opened it. A note was written on the flyleaf inside the front cover. Her tears dropped on the page as she read it.

> *My Dear Miss Curtis,*
>
> *By now you are aware of the profound impression you made on me and have been informed of my actions regarding the same.*
>
> *It would have been a shame for me to do less for I believe that a person of good character should never leave their potential unfulfilled. I am certain my confidence in you is well placed. I only wish I had another lifetime to watch you blossom.*
>
> *I pray that you will live and love your life as much as I have mine. It's a wonderful world for those who are willing to see it as such. With every affection, I ask you to think kindly of me and remember me in your prayers.*
>
> *Yours truly,*
> *Patrick F. Mullock*

It all seemed a lifetime ago to Bertha as she lay in her bed and listened to the ice pans renting and breaking on the shoreline of John's Pond. She could smell the leather binding of the book tucked under her arm. *Captains Courageous* and thoughts of Mr. Mullock were always close at hand. Is this what he expected of her? She was feeling a deep attraction to Napper Darby and, even without Will's comments, it was obvious that he felt the same way about her.

It started as soon as she met him on the road last summer. He being tall and strong didn't make her want to turn away but he was easy going and quick to laugh too. The thing that really captivated her, however, was how he couldn't hide his feelings for her. It was so obvious every time she was near him. He had all the confidence in the world among his friends and neighbours, but turned into a stammering child whenever she showed up.

Still, she wondered what Mr. Mullock would say if he knew Napper. Would he agree that a man like Napper Darby was the right man for her? Napper wasn't rich although he seemed to have enough to make him happy. He was a carpenter and while she was at Littledale she had caught the eye of a couple of chaps who would likely have careers in law or medicine. Will and Mae Kerrivan spoke highly of him and that meant a lot. She would have known soon enough if Will didn't approve of him! She would have to do a lot more thinking about Napper Darby—an anticipation that brought a smile to her face as she snuggled under her blankets.

CHRISTMAS CHEER?

The songs, recitations and skits of the 1903 Christmas concert in the schoolhouse were performed with all the enthusiasm common to such events in small towns. The students' rendition of *The Christmas Story* spread a blanket of goodwill over all in attendance while the two real sheep and the real baby in the cast provided humour not recorded in scripture. After the concert the chairs were pushed back against the walls to clear the floor for dancing—and dance they did.

The floor buckled under the weight of merry-makers keeping step to the fiddle and accordion. Jigs, reels and hornpipes came in fast succession. And then, as the dancers gasped for breath, the musicians launched into 'the lancers'. Around and around the dancers went, 'threading the needle' as the tempo increased and the room swirled into a blur. Finally, just before the some of the revellers were certain to collapse, the players slowed everything down with a waltz. Napper and Bertha never got off the floor.

"Hold me or I might fall down," she said. "I'm so warm."

"You are," he said.

She smiled at him and moved closer. He could feel the curves of her body with every breath she took. She felt tiny in his arms, light and nimble. He had been concerned about making a fool of himself. The only dancing he knew is what he learned in John's Pond. He need not have worried; she made him look better than he was. Too soon the musicians decided to take a break.

"I have to sit down for a few minutes," she said.

"Over here." He led her to chairs in the corner. "I'll get you something cold to drink."

"Just some water, please."

He made his way through the crowd towards where some of the women were serving tea and sandwiches. Before he had a chance to ask for the water he heard the voice of his friend, Ned Keefe.

"Napper, old buddy, how's it going?" Ned was grinning from ear to ear. He had his arm around Kitty Rourke and was clearly enjoying himself.

"Best kind," Napper said. "How about yourself?"

"Couldn't be better." He put his arm around Napper's neck and pulled him close. "Didn't I tell you she was head over heels after you?"

"Yeah, right."

"I did so. Now do you think you can tear yourself away from her for a few minutes?"

"Why?"

"I got something outside I want to show you."

"What is it?"

"You'll never know unless you come out with me."

"What's he up to, Kitty?"

"Shush, darling. Don't tell him a thing," Ned told the girl at his side. She giggled but said nothing.

"All right. Just wait here. I have to get some water first." Napper managed to get a glass of water from one of the women and made his way back across the room to where Bertha sat.

"Will you be OK if I go outside for a minute? Ned says he got something he wants to show me."

"I'll be fine," Bertha said.

"I'll be right back," Napper said as he turned to join Ned who was still waiting where he left him.

"Don't worry, she'll be there when you come back," Ned said. "And you'll wait for me too, won't you?" he said to Kitty as he held her with one arm and put the other around Napper.

"Where are we going?" Napper asked his happy companion.

"All in good time." He let go of Kitty and winked at her. "We'll be back in a couple of minutes, my dear. Don't go anywhere."

Ned kept his arm around Napper's shoulder and pulled him through the door. The cold winter air felt good. More men were cooling off outside. They were quick to comment on Ned and Napper leaving the school together.

"I'd have kept the teacher. Ned won't be as cuddly."

"Did you have to get permission to leave the room?"

"Is she going to keep you after school?"

Napper laughed and shouted to them over his shoulder, "You should have moved quicker fellows. All that any of you can do now is lick your lips."

"Sure, isn't it always the way?" eighty-year-old Clar Bugden lamented to the guffaws of the others.

Ned led Napper up the moonlit lane behind the school. They climbed a fence to get into Paddy Maloney's meadow. A minute later Ned dragged him into a copse of trees in the middle of the meadow.

"You better have something good after dragging me out here tonight."

"Oh, I have. Just wait till I show you." Ned reached behind some scrubby bushes and pulled out a burlap sack. "Look at this—right from St. Pierre." He pulled a half-gallon jar out of the bag.

"You're nuts, Ned. That's what you are, cracked."

"Yeah, I know. Good way to be at times." A dry board lay on the ground. Ned set it across a couple of rocks to make a seat. "Come on, sit down. You can christen it."

"No sirree. I'm not touching that stuff. She'll have a fit."

"Don't be so foolish. She'll never know and what she doesn't know won't hurt her. Go on. Have a small one. It's Christmas." Ned twisted the stopper off the crock and pushed it into Napper's hands. The reek of Demerara rum escaped from the bottle.

"I can't. Not tonight. Where did you get this anyway?"

"Put your ear right there and you can hear where I got it," Ned said. He laughed as he stuck the open end of the bottle to Napper's ear. "It's *parlez vousing* to you. Can you hear it?"

"I can't hear anything you foolish gommel." Napper couldn't help but laugh as Ned pulled the bottle away and put it to his own ear. Bootleg liquor smuggled in from the French islands of St. Pierre et Miquelon was nothing new in John's Pond but it was the last thing on his mind when Ned dragged him away from the dance.

"That's because you don't understand French. Let me listen. Uh huh, uh huh, yeah, that's what I thought. It's saying, 'Share me. Share me with your friend.' Now, be a sport and have a quick one."

"Ned, if she smells rum on me she'll never have anything else to do with me."

"Then we won't let her smell it. We'll have a drop of that soup the women are doling out. She won't smell a thing. Go on, have a little one." He passed the bottle back to Napper.

"I must be nuts to listen to you but if it will keep you happy..." Napper pulled a quick swig and then passed the bottle back to Ned.

Ned pulled back a long draught and wiped his lips. "Here have another one."

"I can't."

"Go on; you can't fly on one wing." Napper took another quick sip and passed the bottle to Ned. "That's better. It's a grand night for a dance isn't it?" Ned took another swallow and passed the bottle to Napper.

Napper felt a pleasant glow in his belly and took a larger swallow. They passed the crock back and forth half a dozen more times. Each helping was more generous than the last.

"When did Kitty Rourke catch hold of you?"

"Oh, she's had her eye on me for a while. She just didn't want to let on—not like the way Miss Curtis chased you." He emphasised 'Miss' so much that they both guffawed at the notion of a teacher flirting at all. Ned tipped the bottle back on his head and took a long swig before shoving it back to Napper.

Napper took the bottle but didn't drink from it. Ned's reference to Miss Curtis had smacked an awareness of duty into Napper's head. "Oh lord, how long have we been out here? I have to get back inside." He stumbled as he stood up.

Ned laughed out loud. "Oh, oh! Careful there, old son. You don't want to fall and spoil your lovely face so the teacher won't kiss it."

"I'll be OK. Don't worry—if I can just make my legs go the right way."

"Hang on. I'll go with you. I'll hide this for later on." Ned put the stopper back on the bottle, wrapped it in the sack and hid it among the bushes. Napper laughed watching his friend stumble as he tried to catch up.

"I think we better get a couple of bowls of that soup."

"Sounds good to me," Ned said, "and some dessert for our sweeties. Oh, life is good. Life is good."

They laughed all the way back to the school. Some men were still outside as Ned and Napper returned. "Looks like you two got another party on the go," one of them said as the lads passed.

"That we have," said Ned, "and it keeps getting better. Right buddy?"

"I suppose," Napper said. "Hang on; wait a minute. We got to get ourselves straightened up before we go in."

"Don't be so foolish. I'm OK. You're OK. The whole world's OK. Isn't that right, fellows?"

"You won't be so OK when Kitty Rourke bares her claws at you," one of the men said to the laughs of his companions.

"I'd say Napper is liable to be kept after school," said another.

Napper's legs wobbled as he went inside. He tried to walk straight but the heat in the crowded hall softened his muscles. He bumped into friends and neighbours as he made his way to where the refreshments were being served.

"Give me a glass of cold water...and some soup," he said to Mrs. Maggie Larkin, one of the servers..

"Napper, are you drunk?" Maggie asked.

"Nooo, not a bit."

"Come over here and sit down before you fall down." She led him to a chair by the wall. "Here's some pea soup. Get it into you. I'll get you a glass of water." She passed him the bowl and a spoon and went for the water.

He slurped a couple of spoonfuls of the soup and stopped. He was warm, too warm. He stared at the crowd trying to locate Mrs. Maggie and the water she promised him. He couldn't see her in the crowd. He stood up to look for her. Something felt warm on his legs.

"Here's your water—Napper, look at the mess you're in. You have soup all over your pants."

"I'll, I'll...clean it. Let me—" He staggered backwards. The wall saved him from falling. Everyone blurred into an unrecognisable mass of faces spinning around the room. "It's awful warm..."

A dry mouth was Napper's first indication that something was amiss. Then he felt the pain, first in his head, then in his back, legs and arms. But it was only when he saw that he was in bed with all of his clothes on that the memory of the night before began to work its way back into his head. He sat up on the edge of the bed and tried to focus. Something was spilled over his clothes. The room stank. He tried to remember. Ned had rum. The dance, Bertha—Bertha, oh no. His stomach rolled and started to heave. He lurched to the window and tugged at the sash but it was frozen shut and wouldn't rise. Puke spewed across the windowpanes. He jammed his hands over his mouth, raced down the stairs and out behind the house.

For the next five minutes he clung to the top fence rail while his insides rolled. After he had nothing left to throw up he convulsed with dry heaves—his stomach working to evict all traces of the sickening matter. Finally he was able to straighten up and look around. He couldn't see anybody. He might have escaped notice. He shivered and his teeth chattered. Every part of his body hurt as he made his way back inside the house but the pain was nothing compared to what was waiting inside. Mrs. Lizzie stood by the stove in the kitchen. The look of disappointment on her face created waves of shame within him.

"Napper, I never expected to live long enough to see you make such a fool of yourself. To be able to bring such a lovely girl to the dance only to turn around and get on the drink—it's beyond me. I never thought I'd witness it."

"I didn't mean to do it."

"Well, for someone who didn't mean to you made a fine job of it—passed out drunk in the corner and having to be carried home."

"Carried—?"

"Yes, carried home. Not that you'd know anything about it." The look on his face confirmed that was the case. "Dave Dollard and Alphie Fuller lugged you out of the hall like a sack of potatoes and brought you home. Thank heavens poor Mike wasn't alive to see it."

The mention of Mr. Mike was a body blow. Napper flopped down on a chair and stared at the floor. Finally he looked up. "Mrs. Lizzie, I'm sorry. You know I never did anything like this before and I'll never do it again."

She wasn't ready to dish out pity. "That's an old song every drunk sings the next morning."

"Mrs. Lizzie, I made an awful mess of everything last night but I have to try to fix it up. I suppose Bertha will never talk to me again."

"If she doesn't you have no one to blame but yourself."

"I know but I have to try."

"You better start by getting cleaned up. Boil a couple of buckets of water and put the washing tub in the back room and take a bath. She won't listen to you the way you reek now."

Napper crammed more thinking into the next couple of hours than into any other part of his life. He had messed up bad, real bad; there was no doubt about it. Bertha might never look at him again but if there was any hope of redeeming himself he had to do something today. As he soaked in the big galvanised washtub he thought about what Mr. Mike would tell him if he were here. His skin was wrinkled from being in the water so long by the time he had it figured out.

"At least you look better now," Mrs. Lizzie said as he came into the kitchen rubbing a towel through his hair. "How are you feeling?"

"I'll live. It's not being sick that bothers me. It's what I did to Bertha. She might never say another word to me."

"That's true but if she's as fond of you as I think she is she might find it in her heart to give you another chance."

"I hope so. Do you think today would be too soon to go see her?"

"Later on this evening. Give her time to get her own mind sorted out."

About three o'clock that afternoon Napper pulled on his coat and cap and set out towards Will Kerrivan's house. With every step he played out in his mind what her reaction might be and how he would respond. His greatest fear is that she wouldn't talk to him at all. He didn't meet anyone on his walk but felt like he was being watched from every window in the place. He was sweating in spite of the cold. Just as he stepped off the road on to the lane leading to the Kerrivan's door a voice roared at him from the woodshed behind the house.

"Where do you think you're going?" It was Will Kerrivan, someone he hadn't factored into his plans.

"I want to talk to Bertha."

"Do you now? You haul your arse in here and talk to me first." Will's teeth were clenched and the squint of his eyes told Napper that his anger was real. Will Kerrivan was not a man to be trifled with when he was angry. Napper took care not to meet his eyes as he stepped into the shed.

"I can't believe you got the gall to show your face around here today after making a fool of that lovely girl last night. I've a bloody good mind to take you out behind this shed and beat some sense into you myself. What the devil were you thinking?"

"Will, I wasn't thinking. If I'd been thinking I never would have done it."

"Do you know what you did last night?"

"I got drunk."

"You got drunk." Will spit a stream of tobacco juice at Napper's feet. "You don't know what you did last night but I'm going to tell you." He barred the doorway with his arm while he talked. "Do you know when Bertha started to get ready for that dance?"

Napper shook his head and muttered, "No."

"About two weeks ago. She's been running around like a little girl trying to make up her mind about what to wear. She spent as much time dolling herself up for you as she did getting the youngsters ready for the concert."

"I had no intention of going drinking. Ned said he had something to show me and pestered me until I went with him."

"Oh, well now that explains it. Now it all makes sense. Come on. Let's go find him."

"Find who?"

"Ned Keefe. I'll straighten him out for spoiling the dance on Bertha."

"Now Will, Ned didn't spoil the dance…"

"Didn't he make you drink? Didn't he pester you until you went with him? Did he lift the bottle to your mouth?"

"I'm the one who drank it. Ned only…"

Will reached for Napper and grabbed the front of his coat. He pinned the younger man to the wall and stood so their faces were only inches apart. "Let's get this straight once and for all. Whose fault is it that you were drunk last night, yours or Ned Keefe's? Or was it someone else? The fellow that made the rum or maybe the sailor that brought it here or was it the devil himself that tipped your head back and poured the booze down your throat?"

"OK. It was my fault."

"You got that right sonny and don't you ever forget it. Nobody else made you do what you did." Will released him and sat back against a sawhorse. "She's thought about nothing for days except how she could be just right for you and what did she get for her trouble? An idiot who thought more about a crock of booze than he did of her."

"That's not true, Will. I think the world of—"

Will roared again. "Shut that hole in your head before I shut it for you. If you think so much of her why the hell did she came home bawling her eyes out. I've a mind to kick your arse right back to Lizzie Fleming's." This time Napper looked him straight in the eye.

"I'd tell you to do that if it would make things better. You got every right to be off the head with me and so does she but tell me one thing, did you expect me to get drunk last night?"

"You'd have never gotten near her if I did."

"That's right. What you saw last night is not what anyone expected from me. No one ever saw it before and, please God, no one will ever see it again." Napper could see that Will was hearing him. "I'd change what I did if I could but I can't. All I can do is promise Bertha I learned from it and it won't happen again. That is if you'll let me talk to her."

"It's up to her who she talks to." Will turned away from Napper and spat another stream of tobacco juice out through the shed door. Napper could see the veins swelling in his neck as he pondered what to do next. He turned and faced Napper. "I'll tell her you're here. If she wants to see you it's all right with me. But if she doesn't, you take your leave with no fuss. Understand?"

"Yes, sir."

Although neither Will nor Napper knew it there was no need to announce Napper's visit. Bertha and Mae heard Will confront him. They couldn't make out what was being said in the shed but there was no doubt about the topic or Will's stand on it. Both of them retreated to the front parlour as Will left the shed and came into the house. He took a couple of deep breaths before he spoke to Bertha.

"Napper's here. He wants to talk to you. You don't have to listen to him. I'll banish him right now if you say so."

"What do you think I should do?"

Will took off his cap and looked at Mae before replying. "He's a good man who did something stupid. I just laid it on him pretty thick out in the shed. He must think a lot of you to find the guts to face me and then you with the state he's in today." Bertha smiled at her protector. "I'd let him have his say. You're not bound by it."

"Tell him to come in."

Napper murmured a heartfelt 'thank you' skyward when Will appeared in the door and beckoned him to come in. Will and Mae were standing in the kitchen. Neither spoke but Will indicated with a nod of his head that Bertha was waiting in the front parlour. Mae closed the parlour door behind him. Bertha was sitting in Will's armchair and although her eyes met his as he entered she didn't speak. He tried to wet his lips but the rest of his mouth was also dry.

"Thank you for seeing me. I came here to tell you two things. The first one is that I'm sorry." He couldn't tell from her expression if his apology meant anything. "What I did was wrong. You deserve to be treated better. I showed no respect and…well, I'm sorry."

He paused for a few seconds and was about to continue when she spoke. "You had two things to say?"

"Uh, yes. Yes I did. I was the happiest man on earth when you said you'd go to the dance with me. I hardly thought about anything else since. Then I made a fool of myself and, what's worse, I hurt you." He shuffled from one foot to another. "I did something last night that I never did before and if, sometime down the road, you can find it in your heart to give me a second chance—I know I don't deserve it—I'll never do anything to hurt you again."

"Is there anything else?"

"No, no that's all. Thanks for hearing me out." He turned to leave.

"Wait, come back." She stood up as he turned towards her. "I didn't know if I wanted to see you or not but now I'm glad I did. Come over here and sit down." She took him by the arm and led him to the sofa. "You hurt me last night—"

"I know. I'm sorry—"

"—but I'll get over it. Napper, a few years ago a wonderful man made a big difference in my life. He did it, and was able to do it, because he was a good judge of character. He said he saw a lot of himself in me." She reached for his hand and held it. "I'm not sure how good of a judge I am but I have complete faith in Will. He says that what I saw last night wasn't the real Napper Darby. He says the real man is the one who had the courage to come here today and face him and then me."

"Well, to be honest, I never thought about having to deal with Will. If I did I might have lost my nerve." Her laugh stirred the same feelings he felt when they first met. He thought for a moment and then looked into her eyes. "Can I say something else?"

"Go ahead."

He took a deep breath. "This time yesterday I didn't know what to be doing with myself just thinking about going to the dance with you and—I hope this comes out the way I want it to—there's something about you that makes me think we were made for each other. I felt it since that day I met you on Whitbourne road and I—"

"Napper, stop talking—"

"—I'm sorry. I didn't mean to—" He stood up but she didn't let go of his hand.

"Stop talking and stay still." She stood in front of him, put her hands behind his head, pulled him close and kissed him. When their lips parted she smiled and said, "Last night is behind us. Let's look ahead."

Their next kiss might have lasted forever if Mae Kerrivan hadn't interrupted it by tapping on the parlour door before opening it. She looked from one to the other and smiled as she asked, "Is Napper staying for supper?"

"Yes, yes he is," Bertha said. "He might even take me out for a walk afterwards."

Napper did take Bertha for a walk that evening and on many evenings after that. He was at her side in church on Christmas morning and he and Mrs. Lizzie ate their Christmas dinner with the boisterous Kerrivan clan. Bertha came to Mrs. Lizzie's for supper. It was a great Christmas season. Times were good that year in John's Pond. The mill sold all the lumber it could put out. All hands had a dollar in their pockets. The twelve days of Christmas saw a constant stream of people visiting from one house to another. Even the weather was perfect with light snow at night and clear frosty days. The Christmas of 1903 stayed fresh in Napper's memory for the rest of his long life. Two things made it so.

It was the Christmas that he fell in love and, even better, had Bertha fall in love with him. In the decades ahead he was quick to counsel young couples that the feelings they have during this time of their lives should be treasured forever because they would never be surpassed.

It was also the Christmas from which he took a great lesson that set him apart from so many of the rest of us. He came to understand, at a far younger age than most, that the world and the people in it are best enjoyed when we have full use and control of our senses. He rarely spoke of it but by his example he showed generations of John's Pond folks that strong drink was not needed to experience the absolute joy of the Yuletide.

One thing was for certain; by the time the Christmas season ended everyone knew that Napper Darby and Bertha Curtis belonged to each other forever.

A PROMISE IS MADE

The end of the Christmas season marked the time for the men of John's Pond to go in the woods for the winter. They would spend the next three or four months cutting logs in the backcountry. They lived in log cabins, camps they were called, for weeks at a time. Some didn't come home until they drove the logs down the river in April. Napper didn't need to go logging; he could have found enough carpenter work to keep busy but he enjoyed the woods too much to stay home.

He and Ned had a camp in Dobbin's Bottom near plenty of logs. The camp was only about an hour's hike from John's Pond so it was no problem for both of them to leave the woods Saturday evening to spend Saturday night and Sunday with Bertha and Kitty. Mrs. Lizzie Fleming adored Bertha and was happy beyond belief that Bertha and Napper were so smitten with each other. Most Saturday nights, after Napper got home and cleaned up, he met Bertha at Will Kerrivan's. She usually had an invitation for them to go to someone's house for a cup of tea. Since she was the teacher and they were a young couple courting the cup of tea always turned out to be the best food in the house served on the good dishes and the finest tablecloth. Often more friends showed up and the night was passed with stories and songs. On a couple of occasions the fun moved outdoors with bonfires and sleigh-rides in the frosty winter night. Their Sunday routine was established early in their courtship. Meet at the church and then back to Mrs. Lizzie's for Sunday dinner before Napper got ready to go back in the woods. One of those Sundays in the winter of 1904 happened to be Valentine's Day.

"Mrs. Lizzie, Ned doesn't like me when I tell him this in the camp but he'll never be as good a cook as you," Napper said as pushed his chair away from the table.

"I don't think you or Ned will ever amount to much as cooks," Bertha said. "I believe the two of you come home every week to eat enough to get through the next week."

"Well, I know one thing for sure," Mrs. Lizzie said to Bertha, "I'm glad that Napper has you to look after him when I'm gone. He'd starve to death if he had to tend on himself."

"Now, what makes you think that Bertha is going to cook for me?" Napper said.

"Well, you know she'll look after you once you're married."

Napper looked at Bertha who smiled and stared at the floor.

"Who said anything about getting married?" Napper asked.

"You know you two are getting married. Sure, you're made for each other. Don't tell me you haven't talked about it?" She looked at Bertha.

"Well no, Mrs. Fleming. The topic has never come up."

"Is that a fact? Oh my, I shouldn't be interfering but, Napper, today is Valentine's Day. Maybe there's something you should be talking to Bertha about before someone else does."

Napper looked from one to the other. They were all laughing by then. "Did you two plan this?"

"Napper, you know I'd never do that," Bertha said. Then she leaned over and whispered in his ear, "but I noticed while we were waiting to eat that Mrs. Lizzie has a new calendar hanging in the parlour." Her broad smile and dancing blue eyes gave Napper the courage to take the calendar off the wall and lay it on the table.

They circled Saturday, the fifth of November 1904.

Napper waited until they were back in the camp later that evening before he broke the news to Ned. His friend was a bit bewildered at first but later, as they lay in their bunks, he seemed to have warmed to the idea.

"Tell Bertha I'll look after the refreshments for the wedding dance."

"I don't think she's going to allow that to happen, Ned."

Two weeks later, on the first of March, Napper and Ned were working on a ridge above Dobbin's Bottom. They had about fifty logs cut and piled when they stopped to boil the kettle and have lunch. They were stretched out on some green boughs drinking their tea in the late winter sunshine when a young fellow about fourteen years old came trotting in the path. He spotted the smoke from their fire and hurried to them.

"Napper, Miss Curtis sent me to get you. You have to go home. Mrs. Lizzie died this morning."

Napper was numb all the way out the trail. According to the young fellow Mrs. Lizzie complained that she wasn't feeling well the previous day. When the neighbours went to check on her this morning she was barely alive and died within an hour. A crowd had gathered by the time Napper reached the house. She was already laid out in a coffin in the parlour. Napper couldn't help but notice the calendar still hanging on the wall above her.

Mae Kerrivan wrapped her arms around Napper's shoulders as he stood staring into the coffin. "It's all right, Napper. She was so excited about you and Bertha getting married she had to go tell Mike all about it."

The people of John's Pond buried Mrs. Lizzie Fleming next to Mr. Mike in the graveyard on the hill. Eight months later they all came together again to marry Bertha Curtis to Napper Darby.

Napper stretched out on the couch with a smile on his face. It was past eight o'clock and Bertha was still fussing about the house.
She glanced towards him and laughed. "Why have you got that silly grin on your face?"

"I like watching you. Come here and sit down. You know there isn't anything left to do."

"I know but it's Christmas Eve and it's our first Christmas together. I want it to be special."

"It is special." He stood up, put his arms around her, and kissed her. Then he picked her up and carried her towards the couch. She wiggled and twisted trying, not very hard, to escape from his arms.

"Put me down. Somebody might see in through the window."

"So what? We're married and I love you all to pieces and you love me just as much."

"Says who?"

"Says you, every time you're able to take your lips away from mine long enough to talk."

"Then it looks like you won't be hearing it very often." She sealed her lips on his and pushed him down on the couch. He was easy to push.

"Having fun?" he asked.

"Starting to," she said. Everything about her excited him— the sparkle of her eyes, the sweetness of her lips, the music of her voice, the allure of her scent, the curves of her body. Then the outside door opened and footsteps could be heard in the porch. They both jumped up.

"Anybody still awake in here or are all hands gone to bed?" It was the unmistakable voice of Ned Keefe. He looked from Napper to Bertha as he entered the kitchen. Kitty was with him. "I was just saying to Kitty that it'd be an awful thing if the two of you were all alone on Christmas Eve with no one to keep you company. I said, in keeping with the spirit of the season, we had to make the effort to come and spend an hour with you."

"Blame him, not me," Kitty said.

Napper extended his hand to Ned, "Merry Christmas, buddy." He bussed Kitty on both cheeks. "Merry Christmas. Come in and sit down."

Bertha hugged Kitty and then stood in front of Ned. "I know you're Napper's best friend."

"Second in his heart only to you, my dear."

"Which is the only reason I put up with you."

"That, and the fact that you are a truly gracious lady."

"As long as we understand each other."

"We do. Now, where's my Christmas kiss you gorgeous thing?" He wrapped his arms around Bertha and dipped her backwards over his knee. Startled, and to stop from falling, she grabbed hold of Ned's ears.

"OWW!"

"Let me up!"

"Let go! You're stretching them!"

"Let me up!"

Napper collapsed in laughter. Kitty fell on a chair barely able to get her breath. In between fits of laughter Bertha poked Ned in the shoulder with her forefinger. "Now there's a Christmas kiss you'll remember, won't you?"

Ned went to the looking glass hanging on the wall. "Look, she did stretch them. They weren't like this when I shaved this morning." He looked at Napper. "You got yourself a handful."

"You better believe it," Napper said as he stood behind Bertha and drew her close.

After the laughter settled down Ned and Kitty shared the real reason behind their visit. "You two look so happy that we decided to set a date for ourselves. We have to build a house first but we should be ready by the last Saturday in October. It's the twenty-eighth."

The young couples shared their plans and dreams until after midnight. Napper and Ned resolved to cut enough logs to get the lumber to build Ned's house. Napper assured him that they would get plenty of help from friends and neighbours to get the job done by the planned date.

After Ned and Kitty left Napper looked at Bertha and said, "Now, see what we started. There won't be a single young fellow left in the place."

"Imagine that, all the young men in one place being so happy. Now, I've got a special Christmas gift for you." She put her arms around him and hugged him.

"What is it?"

"You have to come to bed to find out," she said as she kissed him and turned to the stairs."

"I'll be right up," he said. It took him only a minute to hook the outside storm door, bank the stove and blow out the lamps. He took the stairs two steps at a time but stopped when he reached the bedroom door. The moonlight streaming through the window lit up their bed. Her blond hair cascaded over the pillow and shimmered in the still light. She smiled and turned down the blankets on his side of the bed.

"Why are you just standing there?"

"Because you look like an angel."

"I'm an angel with a gift. Remember? Come to bed."

He lay beside her and wrapped his arms around her. She clung to him "Where's my present?" he asked.

"Well, it's not really ready, yet."

"What do you mean?"

"You know how you keep telling me that you can't believe how you have me all to yourself?"

"Yeah."

"You better enjoy it because it's soon going to end."

"What are you talking about?"

"I'm telling you that this is the last Christmas you'll have me all to yourself...daddy."

Napper was up before the sun on Christmas morning. He went to the stable to feed the horse, cows, chickens and sheep. After the animals were tended to he stepped into the yard and stopped in the early dawn light. He stood with his hands in his pockets gazing around John's Pond. The only movement was the smoke rising from the chimneys. Not a sound moved through the air but he wanted to yell as loud as he could. They were going to have a baby. No one else knew—only him and Bertha. He felt his own heart beating. It frightened him. His eyes moved up the side of his house to the window of the bedroom where Bertha was asleep.

"Dear God, let this all work out right," he murmured.

Inside he made shavings and put them on top of the few embers still glowing in the kitchen stove. The kindling started to crackle right away. He filled the kettle from the water bucket and put it on the stove. The teapot held tea leaves from the night before so he rinsed it and laid it on the top warmer until the kettle boiled. When the kettle was done he poured boiling water into the teapot and sprinkled in a couple of spoonfuls of fresh tea. He laid the teapot on the corner of the stove and sat down on the couch while the tea steeped. He looked around. Bertha's touch was everywhere from the arrangement of the furniture, to the pictures on the wall, to the decorations that brightened every corner. He heard her stirring overhead and then her footsteps on the stairs. She came into the kitchen wrapped in a quilt.

"I was cold." She opened the quilt and wrapped it around him as she sat in his arms.

"The fire is going good. It'll be warm soon."

"I'm all right now. I just need to keep you wrapped up with me."

"OK, but only for a few days. Do you want to open your Christmas present?"

"Not if I have to let go of you. Do you want to open yours?"

"You are mine, you and our baby." He put his hand on her belly.

"You can't feel anything yet. Not for another couple of months."

"I know, but I want the baby to know I'm here."

"Napper, will it always be this good?"

He lay back on the couch so that she lay on top of him. Her head rested on his chest. He stroked her hair while he talked. "Christmas morning is one time of the year when everything seems perfect. Everyone is happy. No one worries." He kissed the top of her head. "I promise you from now until the day I die I'll do everything I can to make every minute of your life feel like Christmas morning."

"Nobody can do that."

"We'll see. We'll see."

FAMILY MAN

The months ahead were a time of wonder for Napper. Bertha went from being his partner to becoming the essence of his life. Month by month he watched her change. Being in a family way, and in keeping with the standards of the day, she resigned as teacher at the end of the school year. He knew how much she loved to teach but she showed no regrets. Her girlish figure disappeared as her body rounded with their child but to him she appeared even more beautiful. She seemed to glow with an aura he could not explain. She laughed when he tried to describe it to her but made him hold her close and tell her about it again. As the winter warmed into spring and then brightened into the long soft days of summer their love deepened into an awesome bond that guided every movement of their lives.

Napper was soaked in sweat turning out barrel staves in the cooper shop at the mill on a hot afternoon in late July when Will Kerrivan tapped him on the shoulder. "You're coming down to the house for supper. Me and you have to fend for ourselves this evening."

"How come?"

"Mae just sent word that she's over at your place. Bertha's gone into labour."

Napper didn't say another word. Before Will could stop him he lit out for home. He crossed two meadows and jumped three fences without losing a stride on the way. He caught a glimpse of Mae Kerrivan standing by the stove as he passed through the kitchen and bolted up the stairs. He slowed down at the bedroom door and peeped inside. The room was empty. He raced back down the stairs.

"Bertha, where are you? Mae, where's Bertha?"

"I'm right here," she said from the parlour. She was holding her belly and trying hard not to laugh. It wasn't working.

"Why are you up walking around? Will said you were in labour."

"I am but that doesn't mean I can't walk. It's going to be a while yet before the baby comes."

"How long?"

"It's not up to me. It's up to the baby."

"And the first one never rushes," Mae said.

"Mae, is it OK for her to be walking around?"

"She's been doing it all her life and it never hurt her." Both of the women were laughing at him.

"When did it start? How long have you been here?"

"It's been a few hours now," Mae said. "Stop worrying. She's doing just fine."

"Ooh," Bertha gasped and clutched her belly.

"Another one?" Mae asked. Bertha nodded.

"Another what? Is she all right? Do you want me to do anything?"

"I told you she's fine," Mae said. "Now, here's what I want you to do. Give her a kiss and go back to work. After work, go to our place with Will and stay there until I send for you." She took Napper by the arm and led him to Bertha. "She's in good hands. Now, be on your way."

He put his arms around Bertha and kissed her. "You'll be all right? I'll stay if you want me."

"I'm OK. Mae is looking after me. You go now and let me have our baby."

Both of them watched Napper walk out the road towards the mill. Mae turned to Bertha and laughed, "Did you hear him? He said, 'I'll stay.' One thing is for sure, my dear, there'll never be a place for a man where a child is being born."

The hours at work that evening were long ones for Napper. It didn't help that the workers in the mill did everything they could to keep him on pins and needles.

"Any word yet?"

"How's the diaper practice going?"

"I saw a young fellow running through the mill yard a few minutes ago; did Mae send him to get you?"

"Is she having twins?"

Will was at Napper's side when the mill saws shut down at six o'clock. Napper looked at him. "I think I'll make a run in to the house, just to see how she is, before I go with you."

"That's why I'm here waiting for you—to make sure you come with me now. Bertha is going to be fine."

"You think I'll be in the way?"

"Nope. You won't be in the way because Mae will throw you out. Rather than put yourself through that why don't me and you cook up a feed for ourselves and bide our time?" Napper gave in and followed Will home.

Once they reached the Kerrivan's house they took a few minutes at the washstand in the porch to rinse the sawdust off their hands and faces. With that out of the way they set about cooking supper. Will had cut up a dried salt codfish before he went to work that morning and left it in a pot of fresh water to soak. He changed the water and put the pot on the stove to boil. Napper went out to the garden and pulled up a couple of potato stalks from which he plucked a dozen potatoes. He washed them and put them in the pot 'with the jackets on'. In the meantime, Will sliced two onions and cut half a pound of salt pork into strips. He rendered out the pork in the frying pan and then fried the onions in the pork fat. Napper cut six thick slices of home-made bread and laid it on the table along with a bowl of fresh butter from the pantry. After another trip to the pantry for a jar of molasses they sat back and waited for the fish and potatoes to cook. Twenty minutes later Will declared it ready. Napper drained the water from the fish and potatoes and shared the lot of on two plates. Will poured the salt pork rashers, grease and onion mixture over the fish and potatoes and they dug in.

"That wasn't half-bad if I do say so myself," Will said fifteen minutes later as he pushed his chair back from the table.

"That's the first feed of salt fish and potatoes I've had since Mrs. Lizzie died," Napper said. He looked out the window towards home.

"Don't be worrying. She's all right."

"I hope so."

"She is. Mae is after bringing a good many youngsters into the world. She'll look after Bertha." Will stretched to shake off the drowsiness brought on by the meal. "Now, how are me and you going to kill the time while we're waiting? I'm going to fall asleep if we don't do something."

"Me too. What needs to be done?"

"Mae's been after me to put a coat of paint on the house. I should put up a few scaffold sticks now while you're here to lend a hand. It'll be a lot easier than doing it by myself."

Will and Napper rigged the scaffold. Friends and neighbours, taking in the summer evening air, stopped by to get the latest news about Bertha and have a chat. Darkness found the two men admiring the sunset from Will's fence.

"It's a beautiful evening," Napper said.

"One you'll never forget."

"No, I don't I suppose I will."

"You won't. You'll remember everything about your youngsters being born especially the first one. Nothing ever happened to you or ever will happen to you again that will change your life so much." Will turned around, leaned his back against the fence and stared at his house. "Your life is not your own anymore. Before you have young ones you can do what you like. Even after you're married the two of you can come and go as you please, but when the little ones show up they call the tune and you dance to it."

"It can't be that bad."

"I never said it was bad. It's the best thing that ever happened to me. I'd never change a thing."

"That's good to hear. I'm nervous enough about this already."

"That's only because it's the first one. After you have seven or eight you'll be the best kind." Napper stared at Will, who laughed and threw his arm around the young man to lead him indoors. "Come on. Let's turn in. I'm expecting an early rise for us."

"I'm going to lie down on the kitchen couch," Napper said. "I'm probably not going to be able to sleep anyway."

"Suit yourself but there's a bed waiting for you and chances are you're missing a good night's sleep. They won't send for you any sooner if you stay awake."

Will blew out the lamps and made his way upstairs. Napper stretched out on the couch and listened to the sounds of a different house. He wasn't sleepy. He stared at the shadows on the ceiling. Bertha's labour started more than ten hours ago. She was enduring pain and risk to bring their baby into the world. The more he thought about it, the more he marvelled at the depth of her love. He was the same now as when he was single. She changed everything to be a wife and mother: her name, her work, her body. Now she was risking her life to have their baby.

He dozed off trying to get his mind around it. It seemed that only moments had passed when he made a sudden jump back to wakefulness but the timepiece showed that it was quarter past two in the morning. He stood up and went to the window. John's Pond was asleep. He saw nothing of interest. Every step he took seemed to make a racket. He was afraid he would wake Will so he went outside. The summer air was warm and still. Bats tweeted overhead. He ambled towards the road and once there began to stroll towards his own place. He knew there was no point going there; Mae wasn't going to allow him in the house. He couldn't go there but he couldn't turn back.

The gravel crunched under his feet. He never realised he made so much noise when he walked. Frogs croaked from a roadside sedge pond. Dogs barked when he passed by a couple of houses but all human activity in the place might have ended for what he saw of it as he made his way through John's Pond. He stopped half way across the bridge and stared down into the water passing beneath it. It was black and silent, moving swiftly, ignoring him, unlike the bright blue water that sparkled and bubbled in the daytime sunlight. It sent a chill through him and made him want to get off the bridge. He walked on into the night towards his home. It was only when he could see his own house that the darkness was broken. Lamplight shone from the kitchen and bedroom windows. He stopped by the roadside instead of going in the lane to his door. He reached down and touched the grass. It was dry so he sat on the sod with his back against a fence post. He made up his mind to stay there until dawn. He would go back to Will's if nothing happened by then.

The silence of the night brought on drowsiness. He dozed. A mosquito buzzing around his ear disturbed his rapture. He slapped at it but could still hear it. He swatted at the air with an open hand. The noise wouldn't go away. He opened his eyes and was startled to see a new day breaking. He must have been asleep for a couple of hours. The noise was still there. It confused him. Slowly he realised that it wasn't an insect. He listened to locate its source. It came from his house. The bedroom window was open now. He stood and listened for another few seconds to be sure he wasn't mistaken about the sound and then ran to the house. This time he stopped outside and took a deep breath before he entered. Nellie Critch was in the kitchen. She beamed when she saw him. "Come upstairs." She took him by the arm and led him to the bedroom door. Mae Kerrivan saw him coming and stood aside for him to enter. Bertha smiled when she saw him. He stopped and stared. A new-born baby nuzzled her breast.

"Come, hold your son," she said. She wrapped the infant in a blanket and passed him to his father. Napper and Bertha laughed as the baby sucked noisily at the side of his own fist. Napper kissed him on the forehead and laid him back in his mother's arms. He knelt on one knee to be close to Bertha.

"He's beautiful," he said. He ran the tip of his finger over the baby's cheek. "What will we call him?"

"I was thinking Michael Patrick, after Mr. Mike and Mr. Mullock."

"Michael Patrick Darby. His name is bigger than he is. I like it."

NOT HOW IT WAS PLANNED

N apper looked forward to the Christmas of 1905 more than any Christmas before. It was Mikey's first and Napper spared no effort to make it one to remember. The fact that the little fellow was too young to remember anything didn't cross his mind. By mid-November the last log was sawed and the mill was shut down for the winter. Napper split his days between enjoying his son and working in his shed. Mikey was growing fast and was getting to know the world around him. The sound of Napper's voice put a toothless grin on his face and set his arms and legs flailing. While the child slept Napper worked. He had built a crib while Bertha was expecting but that was before he had any experience with fast growing babies. It was now clear that while it was fine for a newborn it was too small for a robust youngster to grow up in. He set out to build a better one.

First he found a nice straight spruce on the bank of the river near a place called the Crow's Nest. He cut it into thirty-inch lengths that he then ripped into fifty sticks, each about an inch square. He shaped the sticks, one by one, on a lathe to make the spindles for the side-rails. The panels on each end were birch, hard to saw, harder to shape, impossible to wear out. Years earlier Mr. Mike had come into possession of a dozen oak planks that had been salvaged from a wreck near St. Shott's. The wood lay unused in the corner of the shed for more than two decades. It was the toughest stuff Napper ever worked with but he persisted and it eventually formed the frame that held the baby. But it wasn't just the construction that consumed his time. It was the detail. He would only use unblemished wood. Every piece had to be perfect. He set the same standard for his own labour. Each cut, every joint had to be seamless. The routing on the panels, the lathe work on every spindle had to be without flaw. He sanded and polished until it was as smooth to touch as Mikey's skin.

Bertha had no idea he was building it. When it was done to his satisfaction he covered it with a tarp and put it in the corner of the shed. It would be a nice Christmas Eve surprise. He then set to making a couple of dancing masters. All children loved the little wooden men with the loose joints that could be made to dance a jig while someone sang a ditty. Indeed, few adults could resist picking up a dancing master and breaking into, "di de diddle didle dum" while tapping a rhythm on the puppet's support stick.

In early December he took the pieces of the nativity scene down from the shed loft. He tended to the few repairs that were needed and set up the display in the front yard. Between Mikey's feedings and washings Bertha baked Christmas goodies and put the house in shape for the great season. A stream of neighbours came by to see the baby and offer advice to the new parents.

"What's on your mind?" Bertha asked Napper as they lay in bed on a frosty night the week before Christmas.

"I'm going to get the Christmas tree tomorrow and I'm just trying to think about what else needs to be done."

She cuddled in to him. "Everything is fine. It'll be a perfect Christmas as long as Michael is happy and we have each other. Hold me."

He wrapped his arms around her and pulled her close. Within minutes she was asleep in his arms. He lifted his head and peered over her to the crib where Mikey lay sound asleep. He rolled to his back and stared at the ceiling. The windowpanes were already frosted over in spite of the fact that he banked the stove with birch junks before he came to bed. The boards in the old house creaked and rented in the cold. Sometimes it sounded like a hammer hitting the clapboard. He dozed off knowing a clear, frosty night was a good sign for a fine day tomorrow.

He seemed to be just asleep when more noise from the house worked its way into his slumber. "It can't be that cold," he thought. The noise grew louder. A strange light flickered on the hall ceiling. He sat upright and then scrambled over Bertha towards the baby's crib. "Oh God, Bertha, get up! Get up! The house is on fire! Get up!"

She leapt from the bed and collided with him. He grabbed her by the arm and dragged her towards the door. "Come on. We have to get out!"

"Where's Michael? Napper, I can't find him! I can't find him! Help me!" She broke away from him and stumbled back to the crib. She pawed through the blankets but her baby wasn't in it.

"I got him. Come on. We got to get out! Hold on to me!" He grabbed her again with one hand. Michael was in his other arm. Waves of heat and smoke met them in the stairs. He heard her scream over the roar of the flames. The kitchen was a wall of fire. He dropped to his knees and pulled her down. Keeping the baby tight to his chest he crawled towards the front door and away from the inferno in the kitchen. It was almost impossible to breathe as he felt his way to the front porch. He pulled on the knob, but it wouldn't open. It was locked. The key was on the shelf in the kitchen.

"Take the baby!" He shoved the child into her arms and put his back against the wall. He turned so he could bring his feet to bear on the door. With every ounce of his strength he kicked and kicked the door with both feet. It gave way and he pushed Bertha and Michael outside. They fell to the ground in the front garden. Flames burst through the windows and lit up the night. He saw the terror in her face as they ran out the lane to the road. Michael was crying. They stopped on the road and looked back at their home.

"What will we do? What will we do?" she asked between sobs.

"Is Mikey OK?"

She looked at the baby. "Yes, I think so. He's cold."

"Come on. We have to get help."

The closest house was a quarter of a mile away. They ran there in their bare feet, her in a night-dress, him in long-johns, carrying a baby crying with the cold. Napper pounded on the door until it opened it and they were pulled in from the darkness. The rest of the night was a blur. Everybody in John's Pond showed up in the next few minutes. Mae Kerrivan appeared and took Bertha and Michael. Someone gave Napper clothes. He wanted to go back to his house to help put out the fire. Ned Keefe sat him down and told him to stay where he was.

"It's too late. Let it burn out. We'll build a new one."

Hours later, in borrowed clothes, Napper shivered in the grey morning and stared at the ashes of his home. Light snow dusted the ground around the smouldering ruins. The patch of black looked tiny. Only the stove and chimney were recognizable. A dozen men and a handful of curious youngsters milled about. Ned Keefe stood by his side as he had all night.

"It's hard to look at now," Ned said, "but I guarantee you it'll be a lot easier to stand here this time next year." It was umpteenth assurance that Ned had given his friend.

"I can't believe it's all gone. It happened so fast. We got nothing."

"You got Bertha and the baby. You'd call this a good deal if we were getting ready for a funeral. You'll make out OK."

"Yeah, I know, but still…"

"But nothing. If this were someone else's house you'd be the first one to tell them not to worry. You know as well as I do that the first logs cut this winter will be yours and you won't be driving nails by yourself."

Napper reached for Ned's arm and turned his friend so he could look into his eyes. "This is my fault. I must have left the draft open when I banked the stove for the night."

"Don't start that foolishness," Ned said. "Maybe you did start it. Maybe you didn't. There's no way to know." He pointed to the ashes. "What difference does it make? It's behind us and we can't back up. We'll build a new one."

"I don't expect everyone else to provide for me. It's not what I'm used to."

"You never expected a fire either but you got it. We've always been told that we have to take the bad with the good. Well, you got the bad so you can look forward to the good. Now, do you and Bertha know where you're going to stay?"

"Not yet."

"Well, me and Kitty want you to move in with us. I'll have a bed set up for you before supper time."

"Thanks. I'll tell Bertha. Chances are though that Will and Mae already moved her back in with them. I have to go over to Will's and see how she's making out. I hardly spoke to her since this started."

"I'll go with you. Kitty is going to be asking about her and the baby."

The men at the fire scene delayed them for another hour re-assuring Napper and telling him that he would have all the help he needed. He was feeling the load lighten from his shoulders as he walked to Will Kerrivan's. Ned kept up a steady banter as they moved.

"It's a funny thing, you know," Ned said.

"What is?"

"Remember last Christmas Eve when me and Kitty showed up at your house?"

"And Bertha stretched your ears?"

"Yeah, she did stretch them too. Look, they're still not back the way they were." Ned lifted his cap and shoved his ear towards Napper.

"Put your cap back on, you foolish gommel. What about last Christmas?"

"You were the one telling me it would be no problem to build a house a few months. Remember?"

"I know. It's a queer thing how the world changes isn't it?"

"Nothing changed. You lost an old house and a bit of furniture. It can all be put back. Keep that in mind when you're talking to Bertha."

"I'll try."

"She'll feel better if she believes you can work your way through this and you know you can."

Bertha was wrapped in a quilt in the kitchen rocking chair with Michael in her arms when Napper and Ned came in. Her eyes were wide as she looked at her husband. Will and Mae were there too. Napper crossed the kitchen and turned down the quilt to look at his son and then glanced at Will before speaking to her.

"There's not much clearing away to do before we can start building."

"Everything's gone?" she said.

He nodded. "Everything in the house."

"What are we going to do?"

"Build a new one. What else can we do?"

"I don't know where to start. We got nothing."

"We got out alive. The shed and stable weren't touched. I still have my tools. The animals are OK."

Will spoke up. "You know got a roof over your heads for as long as you need it too."

"That's right," Mae said. "It's an awful way it happened but I'm delighted to have you here for Christmas especially this little darling." She smiled at the infant in Bertha's arms.

"You can count on everyone in the place lending a hand," Ned said. "How many fellows already said they'd help?"

"Everyone I talked to," Napper said. "Half a dozen even offered to take us in including Ned and Kitty."

"Tell Kitty thanks," Bertha said. "It's sweet of both of you, but Mae already has my old room made up. I don't think we'll be allowed to go anywhere else."

"You got that right," Will said. He nodded towards Napper. "I let him take you out of here once before but you're staying this time until he builds you a new house. I don't care if it takes ten years."

"It won't be ten years," Napper said. "It might be ten months but all of you are invited to our house for Christmas dinner next year."

Will walked across the kitchen and stood behind Napper and Bertha. He put his arms around their shoulders and drew them close.

"We got some busy times ahead of us," he said. "In the meantime, there's no sense being miserable. We'll have a grand Christmas, do what has to be done and move ahead."

Bertha smiled but the smile looked forced to Napper. His mind was already racing with ideas for the new house. She was still trying to cope with the loss. Her troubles bothered him but he remembered something that might cheer her up. That afternoon him and Ned went back to his shed. They put the new crib in a horse-drawn box-cart and brought it to the Kerrivan's house. This time the smile on Bertha's face was genuine. Will Kerrivan stated that it was as fine a piece of craftsmanship as he had ever laid his eyes on.

"Strong enough for a horse and pretty enough for an angel," is how he described it.

Mae watched little Michael kicking his legs and laughing at all the attention he was getting as he lay in the crib for the first time. She put her arm around Bertha's shoulder and squeezed her. "It's a beautiful thing to bring to a new home. A hundred years from now some lucky youngsters will be still sleeping in it."

"I'm turning in," Napper said after he finished his supper. He could hardly stay awake and was asleep almost as soon as his head hit the pillow. A couple of hours later Bertha tried to lower herself into the bed without waking him but he opened his eyes. "How come you're creeping around?"

"I was trying to be nice to you."

"You're always nice to me." He wrapped his arms around her and pulled her close. "Are you feeling better?"

"A little. I never dreamed when I went to bed last night that we'd be sleeping here tonight."

"It's been a rough day for sure but at least the three of us are still together. Everything else can be replaced."

"It's strange, you know. We lost the house but what hurts the most is losing the book that Mr. Mullock gave me."

"Yeah, I know. I've been thinking about some of the stuff belong to Mr. Mike and Mrs. Lizzie too, especially Mrs. Lizzie. I still got a lot of Mr. Mike's stuff in the shed."

"There's not much we can do about it except remember them as best we can."

"I know one thing for sure. If any of them were here they'd be telling us to never mind that stuff and to look after each other. Do you remember the promise I made to you last Christmas?"

"That you'd try to make every day like Christmas? You've done a pretty good job of keeping it."

"I was thinking today when me and Ned were bringing the crib over here that it's easy to make the good days feel like Christmas. It's days like this that test us. There'll be more of these days ahead but I still mean what I said last year."

"You know something Napper?" She kissed him long and hard. "I just lost every scrap I owned but I still have everything I need."

It was bright and sunny when Napper woke the next morning. Never one to sleep in, he was on his feet in a second. It was way past feeding time for his animals. Bertha and Michael were still sound asleep. Downstairs Mae greeted him with a smile.

"Sit down and have your breakfast."

"I can't. I slept in. I have to go feed the horse and sheep."

"My love, Will left an hour ago to go tend on them. He knew you were beat after yesterday and didn't want to wake you. He's likely on his way back by now." She took a plate of toast down from the warmer and laid a mug on the table. "Now sit down and have a cup of tea."

"That was good of Will. I was tired."

Michael must have heard Mae and Napper. He started to cry. Napper stood to go upstairs but Mae stopped him. "Eat your breakfast. I haven't dressed a baby in ages. I'll get him and let Bertha have a rest."

She went upstairs. Napper glanced out the window and saw Will coming in the road. Minutes later he was in the porch taking off his cap and boots.

"It's a grand day out there. How are you feeling this morning?"

"Better," Napper said. "Thanks for letting me sleep."

"It's what getting along in this world is all about."

1906 was to be one of the busiest years in all of Napper's life. Straight away into the new year he took to the woods. It was dark when he left the camp in the mornings. At first light the steel of his axe bit deep. It was dark again before set it in a stump and turned his face towards the camp for the night. Every night he had at least another sixty logs piled alongside the path. When the ice left the river that spring he broke every log jam as soon they started so as not to delay the log drive downstream to the mill. But he didn't work alone. Ned stepped out into the dark with him every morning. When he pulled on a jammed log in the river a neighbour pushed from the other end. He hauled the first load of lumber home from the mill on the last Saturday in May. The second and third loads were right behind him on horse-drawn carts driven by friends.

The sills were laid Monday evening and by nightfall Friday evening the floor was down and the first story framed out. The pace never slacked for the summer and on the first Sunday of October Napper was able to move Bertha and Mikey into a new house built on the ashes of the old one. Everyone in the place dropped by to get them settled in and wish them well but Bertha and Napper were too tired to celebrate and thank them in a proper fashion. They waited until Christmas to do it right.

Bertha cooked up a Christmas dinner the likes of which had never been seen in John's Pond. Everyone in the place was invited to—yes everyone—with hand-written invitations. The house was blocked from the moment church ended on Christmas Day until well past midnight. By the time that Napper and Bertha finally tumbled into bed early on Boxing Day morning they could only smile at each other in contentment

"I think the people in John's Pond set the standard for house warming," Bertha said as she snuggled in Napper's arms. A long, sleepy yawn was his reply.

CHILDREN'S CHRISTMAS

I t was a good thing Napper and Bertha did not scrimp on the size of the new house. It was a square two-story with four bedrooms upstairs. Over the next decade six more babies came into their lives. Elizabeth, named for Mrs. Lizzie, came along two years after Michael. William arrived in the fall of 1908 followed by Joseph in 1910. Then a string of girls showed up, three in a row. Margaret came late 1911, then Ellen. Mary, known to everybody as Minnie, was the youngest. She was born in the summer of 1915.

Napper and Bertha watched the world change as they brought their children into it. By the time Minnie was born a savage war raged across the ocean. Eight local young fellows had signed up to fight for King and Country; more were talking about going. The latest news from the battlefields in France entered every conversation.

By the first week of November in 1915 all the logs were sawed but there was no waiting until after Christmas to go in the woods. The war demanded lumber and it was fetching top prices. David Thistle let it be known that he expected all hands to be in the woods as soon as the mill-saws stopped. There was even talk of starting up the mill in mid-winter if a way could be found to get the logs to the mill yard.

"You're going already?" Bertha said as Napper hauled on his coat. It was only ten minutes earlier that he came home to lunch, a lunch he shoved into his mouth making it almost impossible to talk to her.

"Have to," he said while trying to slurp down the last of a mug of tea without scalding his throat. "We have to take the boom and the cribs out of the river and stowed away today."

"I'm making a pot of stew for supper. Will you be home on time?"

"I should be," he said over his shoulder as he went out the door.

Bertha watched him go, walking so fast that he was almost running. He was always in a hurry these days. She tried to remember the last time that the two of them sat down and had a chat. Minnie started crying.

"Hold on, my sweet. Mommy's here." She wasn't finished feeding and changing Minnie when Ellen came into the kitchen crying because she wanted to play with the same doll as Margaret. Bertha sorted out that spat while pinning the fresh diaper on the Minnie. She sent five-year-old Joey to the root cellar to get carrots, turnips and potatoes for the stew while she cut up the meat. Once the stew was simmering on the stove she went to the clothesline and brought in the clothes she had scrubbed and hung out that morning. She put the kettle on to boil and folded and put away the clothes. It seemed, a few minutes later, as she sat in the rocking chair by the window with her tea that it was the first chance she had all day to rest her feet.

Napper didn't show up until almost seven o'clock. Instead of eating, he lit a lantern and went to the stable to tend to the animals. Then he filled the wood-box and the water buckets before he finally hauled his logans off his feet and came in.

"I'm gut-foundered," he said to Bertha. She took the plate of stew down from the warmer above the stove.

Mikey was sitting on the couch watching his father. He joined Napper at the table. "Dad, me and Bobby Morrissey set a string of snares around Rocky Pond marsh this evening."

"That's a good spot for rabbits," Napper said, "but I don't want you two going beyond there unless I'm with you."

"But you never come with me anymore. You're always busy."

"I know, but I have to work. One thing I shouldn't have to do is bring in wood and feed the horse after I get home. If you're able to snare rabbits you're able to look after that stuff."

"I'll do it from now on. I promise."

Mikey stood close to his shoulder waiting for an acknowledgement but Napper's mouth was full. He needed a few seconds to gulp down his food before he could say anything. In that time his eyes met his son's. He smiled and ruffled the boy's hair.

"Good man. I'll tell you what we'll do. You keep the woodbox full and feed the animals and I'll show you how to make a woof stick."

"A what?"

"A woof stick. It's something Mr. Mike showed me when I was no older than you. I just about drove Ned right out of his mind trying to figure out how it worked."

"You promise?"

"I promise and I never break a promise." He winked at Bertha. "You keep your end of the deal and we'll make the woof stick after dinner Sunday. You'll be able to take it to school on Monday."

"I don't know if taking a woof stick to school is a good idea," Bertha said as she poured tea from the teapot into a mug for Napper.

"That's the teacher in you talking now," Napper said. "It won't be any harm. Mikey's a good boy, aren't you?" The young fellow grinned, clearly enjoying the attention he was receiving.

Two hours later the children were in bed. Napper stretched out on the kitchen couch reading a week-old St. John's newspaper that the mailman brought to John's Pond earlier in the day. Bertha put aside a pair of mitts she was knitting to pour a cup of tea for each of them.

"It seems there are not enough hours in the day or days in the week to get it all done," she said.

"I know. I'd like to be able to spend more time with the youngsters but I can't stop working to do it."

"No one expects you to, my love. Your first job is to provide for us and you're doing a grand job of it. I think that all you need to do is make sure you say a few words to each of them every day. Did you see Mikey's face light up when you paid attention to him?"

"To tell you the truth, it frightened me. I didn't know if I should be proud or ashamed."

"You're working hard to look after your family. That's nothing to be ashamed of."

"I know, but a father shouldn't be a stranger to his children."

"I hardly think they look at you as a stranger."

"Maybe not yet, but if I keep going the way I am I'll be nothing more than a fellow who shows up every evening looking for his supper and a place to fall asleep."

Bertha laid the two cups of tea on the table and then sat on the edge of the couch where he was lying. She nudged aside the newspaper and smiled at him. "I don't have any problem with you showing up here every night looking for a place to sleep and you're as good a father as any man can be. Now, come and get your tea."

Napper sipped on his tea while Bertha recounted the events of the day. He nodded and smiled as Bertha talked about Margaret and Ellen making a bigger mess trying to sweep the floor than if they had left the dust where it was. As she finished her story she looked over the edge of her cup to where he sat across of the table. "Did you hear a single word I said?"

He laughed and put his own cup on the table. "I did, my love. It's just that sometimes I think I'm missing something. It's like the youngsters are growing up and I'm not part of it."

"That's foolishness you're talking now."

"Maybe, but sometimes I think if I were to disappear off the face of the earth tomorrow they'd never know I was gone except at mealtimes."

"Napper, I don't want to hear any more of that kind of talk; your children adore you. Disappear of the face of the earth—where did you ever come up with such an awful notion?"

"Don't worry my darling. I'm not leaving tonight. I'll tell you what it is that I want. I want the youngsters to be able to look back when they are grown up and remember stuff I did with them when they were children."

"You know they will."

"Maybe, but I want to make sure."

"How?"

"I have an idea. I'm going to have it done by Christmas morning."

Napper spent every minute that he could spare over the next few weeks holed up in his shed. The youngsters paid him no attention which suited his purpose fine. Bertha was no wiser about what he was up to than the children. All was revealed on Christmas morning.

Elizabeth was the first to wake and creep downstairs. Her squeals roused the others who tumbled downstairs to see her jumping up and down in the front room. Napper was close behind them. Sitting in the middle of the room was a hand-cat—a huge hand-cat painted green with red trim. One glance was all one needed to know it was a hand-cat far too pretty to use hauling wood. It was built for fun.

"Look at it, Mom! Look! A new hand-cat!" By the time Bertha got downstairs Napper, still in his long-johns, had Margaret and Ellen seated on the big sled. Mikey and Elizabeth had already

looked outside and determined that the snow conditions were perfect. Bertha couldn't contain her excitement.

"Come on. Let's get dressed and go up on the hill," she said.

Joey and Billy were pulling on their outdoor gear. "Wait for us!"

"Mom, where're my mitts?"

"Can we go too, Mom? Can we?" Ellen pleaded.

Bertha, with baby Minnie in her arms gave up trying to make
sense of the pandemonium in front of her and started to laugh.
"Oh, it's beautiful! Be careful! Don't break anything."

"Dad, get dressed and come out with us!"

"OK, I'll be right with you."

Bertha had never seen him happier. She grabbed him by the
arm and kissed him on the cheek. "Get some breakfast first. I'll
dress the baby and come out with you for a few minutes."

Within twenty minutes Napper had finished some toast and
tea, and was dressed for outdoors. Bertha had fed Minnie and
bundled her up and passed her to her father. "Come on my sweet,
let's go have some fun in the snow," he said as he buried his face in
the baby's belly. She giggled and grabbed at his hair. "You're coming out too?" he said to Bertha.

"As soon as I get dinner in the oven." She watched through the
window as Napper made way up the hill carrying Minnie in his
arms. Friends had joined the children. All of them were taking
turns riding on the new hand-cat. They yelled for Napper to watch
them as they made the run down the snow covered slope. They
laughed as he brought Minnie the brink of the hill and then sat
his lanky frame on the front bunk with her in his arms. He held
Minnie while Mikey and Joey pushed them down the hill. Every
youngster on the hill laughed and yelled as he zipped towards the
bottom. Bertha was taking in the scene when, for some reason, the
promise he made to her on their first Christmas together came
into her mind. She remembered telling him that nobody could

make every day be like Christmas Day. She felt a tear trickle on her cheek.

"Nobody else could, but he did." She wiped her face with the back of her hand and pulled on her coat. "I want a ride too," she called as she started up the hill.

That Christmas was probably the one that made people take notice of Napper's extraordinary enthusiasm for the season. Happy children spread the word about the hand-cat through John's Pond.

"He made it just for riding on?" was the usual first reaction, followed by something like, "Him *and Bertha and the baby* were on hill? I'd have paid to see it."

More than a few people viewed Napper as a bit of a strange duck for celebrating Christmas with so much gusto but they changed their minds when they saw that his enthusiasm was real. Soon, not only did the people of John's Pond accept his festivity but they embraced it. In the years ahead Napper could be counted on to bring about something wonderful every Christmas. One year he got all hands together up in his meadow for a bonfire and singsong. (Bertha led the singing.) A few years later he had every horse and slide in John's Pond take part in a sleigh ride to Murray's Pond. Everyone remembered the fun mainly because Napper didn't just do it in the good times; he did it when it was needed most—when good times were hard to come by.

The depression struck here the same way it struck cities like New York. The bottom fell out of the price of lumber. No one could afford it I suppose. If they could afford lumber they couldn't afford the nails to hold it together. The hard times became official in John's Pond when Mr. Dave Thistle stood on the haul-up ramp in front of the mill workers before the saws started in the spring of 1931.

"Men, I'll give it to you straight," he said. "I've been running the mill for more than forty years but it's going to be nip and tuck as to whether or not I can keep going. I'm still not paid for a lot of the lumber we sent to St. John's last fall, and the way things are now, I probably never will be. I can't say when I'll be able to put cash in your hands again but I'll do my best to run a grub account in the store for anyone who wants to stay with me. You'll get credit against your accounts for the logs you cut and your work in the mill."

Not much more needs to be said about Mr. Thistle beyond the fact that not a single man left him, at least not because they felt they were being short-changed. All hands received their staples on account. It was rough grub for sure: flour, tea, molasses and beans made up the bulk of it along with kerosene for the lamps and, every now and then, some sugar for a treat. It wasn't much when we look back but everyone had a vegetable garden and kept hens and sheep. There was fish in the bay along with berries, wild game and firewood from the woods. It wasn't prosperity but it could have been worse.

Anyway, getting back to Mr. Thistle, nobody left him and he didn't cut any jobs but on Christmas Eve in 1932 he did something wonderful to show his appreciation to his workers. Turkeys were never part of the wildlife around John's Pond so they weren't on the Christmas menu either. A couple of wild ducks or a fat Canada Goose would be more familiar fare on the big day. A family coming off a good year might feast on a roast of mutton. Others might make do with a laid-out hen. In 1932 Mr. Thistle let it be known as Christmas approached that he would provide the Yule feast for all. He was true to his word.

The week before Christmas he butchered two fine head of cattle. He cut the meat into portions more generous than anyone would cut for themselves. Christmas Eve morning he and Charlie Bugden loaded the meat into a box cart. Mrs. Thistle then put small gifts of her own in the cart for the women in each house. There was nothing big, just some little ornamental dishes and framed pictures wrapped in bright tissue. "Something to put a bit of colour in Christmas," she said. Mr. Thistle and Charlie hitched one of his Clydesdales, complete with bells, to the cart and Charlie set out. Well, old Charlie Bugden never claimed to be Santa Claus and why would he? Santa never received as fine a welcome at his stops.

"How many have you for dinner tomorrow? Ten! Well now, here's enough for fifteen, and Happy Christmas to you and yours."

"How many are you feeding? Eight! This will do for a dozen, and Happy Christmas to all of you."

"And you ma'am, how many will be at your table? Fourteen! My dear you need a big piece. Here, this will feed twenty for sure, and Happy Christmas to every blessed one of you."

Charlie spread a lot of smiles around John's Pond that day and not only because of the meat and gifts. Most of the men had a drop of home brewed beer or St. Pierre rum stashed away for special occasions and all would agree that having such kindness shown in a year of need was special for sure. A glass, in good spirit, was thrust into Charlie's hands at most houses. By the time he reached Napper's door in the early evening according to Napper, "It was a good thing the horse knew where they were going."

Mr. Thistle's gesture set Napper and Bertha to thinking. Times were bad, but Christmas still came. Their own children were hardy. Michael and Elizabeth were married with children of their own; Minnie, the youngest, was seventeen. They would enjoy the season whether they received gifts or not. Still, a lot of young parents had children waiting for Christmas magic. Napper and Bertha set to work. In the lean years that followed many little boys woke up on Christmas morning to discover a well crafted hockey stick waiting under the tree while a lot of little girls danced with delight to find pretty rag dolls just like ones Bertha first saw at St. Anne's or-phanage. Those few toys along with an apple or an orange in their stockings and an abundance of laughter and hugs became the Christmas memories of the children who grew up in John's Pond in the dirty thirties. Oh, and of course, the sight of Charlie Bugden making his Christmas Eve deliveries. Dave Thistle declared that, no matter the cost, he would never enjoy another Christmas if he didn't see Charlie making his way along the roads and lanes of John's Pond with Christmas dinners for all.

YANKS FOR CHRISTMAS

The dirty thirties ended with a bang. It was the explosion of the worst war we human beings ever started. Like the generation before them John's Pond boys signed up to serve but this time the war struck a lot closer to home for Napper and Bertha. Billy joined the Overseas Forestry Unit. He went to Scotland with three thousand other young men to cut pit-props for the coal mines that kept Britain running. Joey joined the navy and was assigned to a warship escorting convoys across the ocean.

Napper and Bertha spoke proudly and worried constantly about both of them. Joey was still single, although he had a sweetheart. Billy had a wife and four children. His service pay came home and provided for their necessities, but a young family still needed help in other ways. Firewood had to be cut, hay mowed, repairs done around the house and so on. Napper found himself busier than ever.

He was the now the foreman in the mill and made it a point to be there ahead of the other workers every morning. He was often the last one out in the evening. One good thing about being foreman was that he no longer spent his winters in the woods. Instead, he travelled through the ridges and cut-outs every week to scale the logs the men had cut and calculate their value. He even taught himself how to drive the flatbed truck used to deliver the mill's lumber to St. John's and then surprised everyone by buying a used pick-up for himself. After work he tended to his own house, gardens and animals and then did what he could for Billy's wife and youngsters. It was non-stop from before daylight until he fell into bed at night. Still, there were bright spots; one of the brightest was the Yanks coming here.

This part of the world had hardly changed in the four hundred years since John Cabot sailed over from England. Then, with no warning, twenty-five thousand young fellows from all over America showed up and they didn't tiptoe in through the back door. No sir, they marched in and turned the place upside down. They took a look at Argentia, about twenty-five miles from here, and said it was the perfect spot for a navy base. All hands living there had to shift three miles to new homes in Freshwater. Then they figured that the runway should go where the graveyard was so they moved the dead too. Everywhere you turned, all hours of the day and night, trucks and buses were coming and going. New docks were built and lined with ships. Hangars popped up and were filled with airplanes. There was no end to the money. Everyone was either working on the base or working for someone doing business with the Yanks. It was like all hands turned into millionaires overnight.

The Yanks decided to upgrade the road between Argentia and St. John's. They built a barracks right here in John's Pond for eighty-five men to live in—sea-bees they were called. What a nice bunch of men they were. Everyone around here took a liking to them. They were only young fellows. A lot of them were still in their teens and never away from home before. I suppose some of them thought they had landed in another world and they had in many ways. John's Pond had no telephones or electricity but that didn't slow down the Americans. They rigged up generators the first night they were here and that Friday they invited all hands to a movie at their canteen. It was the first movie most John's Pond folks ever had the chance to see. Pretty well everyone showed up although a few were nervous about going because they weren't sure about the hot 'dogs' that the Americans promised to give out. But it wasn't all one sided. We opened our hearts and homes to the servicemen. Friendships grew. They enjoyed their time off fishing and hunting with the local people—although their favourite catch for sure was the John's Pond girls.

On a Sunday afternoon five days before Christmas they invited everyone to their mess hall for a big turkey dinner. They had the place decorated and a huge Christmas tree with coloured electric lights. They played records of Christmas music and even had Santa Claus there with presents for the children. It was a wonderful time, no doubt about it, but as Napper moved among the Yanks it seemed to him that every one of them was talking about home. He let them talk and heard about the Christmas lights of New York City and Christmas dinner in the Blue Ridge Mountains of Georgia. He listened while a young sailor with a Spanish accent told how his Mexican grandparents hung a *piñata* on the patio every Christmas Eve for their grandchildren and nodded with understanding as a Montana cowboy discussed how animals needed tending on Christmas Day just like every other day of the year. None of the men were the same. Their stories were all different; yet, they were all identical.

Napper and Bertha talked about it as they made their way along the road to home a few hours later. Their children were grown and moved out on their own but they all lived within a day's travel of home and all of them, along with the grandchildren, were coming home for Christmas dinner.

"Would it make any difference if there were two or three more at the table?" he said.

"Only two or three?" she said, and linked her arm into his. "What about the rest of them?"

"Did I ever tell you about the time Con Larkin drowned"

"I don't think so. Why?"

"I'm thinking about how Mr. Mike set things right when there was too much work for one person."

Monday morning Napper started telling his friends and neighbours what he and Bertha had in mind. By the end of the day he had arranged for every one of the military men, all eighty-five of them, to be taken in by a family for dinner on Christmas Day. The men knew nothing about it until a list was posted on their barrack's bulletin board telling them what family was expecting them. To say they were astonished wouldn't do justice to their reaction especially when it was made clear they were to bring nothing except appetites and goodwill.

The Christmas celebrations started as usual in John's Pond when Charlie Bugden made his rounds delivering the Christmas roasts. That hadn't changed in spite of the war and Mr. Dave Thistle passing away a few years earlier. His son inherited the business and clear instructions to continue providing the food for Christmas as long as folks appreciated it. The sight of the horse-drawn boxcar and its tipsy driver making sure that all hands had plenty was one of the pleasant memories that many servicemen carried with them when they left John's Pond.

Jefferson Benton from Missouri and Frank Taylor from Chicago joined Napper and Bertha and their family on Christmas Day. Young Benton was a skinny, seventeen-year-old farm boy who said he joined the navy because he never wanted to walk in mud again. Napper pegged him as coming from a family that had seen hard times. Taylor was different. He was twenty-two, a sheltered city boy studying history at the University of Chicago when the war broke out. His father and grandfather were lawyers and expected him to follow in their footsteps but he would not sit in a classroom while his friends signed up to fight. Enlisting caused bad blood between him and his father. The rift widened when he discovered that he loved navy life. The camaraderie was new to him and he enjoyed every minute of it.

They all made their way from the church to the house. The youngsters, armed with toys and dizzy with excitement, chased each other through the house. The women gathered in the kitchen to help Bertha with the food and share comments about the guests in uniform. The men congregated in the front room where Napper had set up a plank table to handle the overflow. Soon the food appeared.

The roast beef that Charlie had delivered fell apart at the touch of a fork. There were carrots and turnips sweetened by the kiss of frost from Bertha's garden, along with peas pudding and boiled figgy duff. Salt beef and pickled beets added relish and it was all topped off with a magnificent fruitcake. The young Americans ate until they were about to burst. Jefferson said that he only wished his brothers and sisters could see the feast that Bertha spread out for them. Frank declared, while sharing the roast beef and partridgeberry crumble with three generations of Darbys, he now knew for sure that riches were not needed for wealth.

Napper smiled when he said it and looked at his children and their children. All of them were full to the brim. All of them had smiles on their faces; so did he. Ellen, sitting at the far end of the table, saw his contentment.

"Dad, you look like you're enjoying this," she said.

"How can I not enjoy something like this, my love? All of you, new friends, lots of food—did you ever stop to think how many people around the world would change places with any of us right now? I only wish that Billy and Joey were here but you can be sure they are thinking about us." Silence fell across the table as he continued. "The whole world is in a rage. Families are torn apart. Countries are destroyed. Everybody is frightened about what's going to happen next. The sad part is that most of the people who are fighting would get along fine if they were able to sit down together. Keep that in mind whenever you don't know what to make of someone. It's easy to walk away and think the worse but if you have a cup of tea with them you'll find that pretty well all of us in this world want the same things: enough to eat, a warm bed and to be close to the ones we love. Sure, I have all of that and more. Why should I be anything but happy? Why should any of us?"

"Here, here!" Frank Taylor said as he broke the silence and clapped his hands. Everyone, much to Napper's embarrassment, joined in.

"Well said, skipper," Michael said to his father, "although I never knew you as one for making speeches."

"I'm not. It's just the way I see things. Now, how many of you young ones are any good to sing? Come on, I want to hear *Jingle Bells.*"

That was the way it was all around John's Pond on Christmas Day in 1942. Everyone had a grand time and, at least for a few minutes, those young fellows from the states were able to forget about the war and enjoy Christmas. They all shipped out in the months ahead and we lost touch. Hopefully, they all made it home safe and sound—although I suspect a lot of them never did.

ANOTHER GENERATION

It was almost another three long years before the war ended and, thank the Lord, Billy and Joey came home in good health. In the decade ahead Napper and Bertha watched the world change with dizzying speed. The Argentia navy base kept growing. Mike and Joey worked with the Americans. So did Elizabeth's husband and their oldest son. Billy operated a big Cat dozer for one of the construction companies building new roads to handle the automobiles that everyone suddenly owned. Ellen, Marg and Minnie all had husbands, homes of their own and children who were having children themselves.

Michael's oldest boy, Jim, was the first to make great-grandparents out of Napper and Bertha. Their little girl, Laura, was born in the spring of 1952, but it was another year before Napper and Bertha saw the child. Young Jim had completed an electrician's course a few years earlier and took it in his head to spend a summer seeing more of the world. He was twenty-two. He left with the intention of travelling three hundred miles to the paper mill in Grand Falls. He ended up two thousand miles away in Toronto working with a construction company owned by an Italian family. The owner's daughter, Gina, worked in the office. Well, there you have it: a fine young man, a pretty young woman and a long, hot summer. To no one's surprise they were married the next June and little Laura was born the following spring. It was impossible for them to visit during the summer because of Jim's work but the three of them landed at St. John's airport the week before Christmas 1953. That night Laura slept in the crib that Napper built for her grandfather.

Gina Darby loved Christmas in John's Pond. Jim had explained to her before they left Toronto that his home was a small village on the edge of the ocean and the forest. He told her only a couple of hundred people lived there and that it hardly changed in a hundred years. The night they arrived Mike's house was blocked with Jim's friends and relatives who had all come to see him and to welcome his wife and child. It was past mid-night when they finally fell into bed.

"This is just like home," Gina said as she cuddled into her husband.

"John's Pond is hardly Toronto," Jim said.

"I'm talking about the people, not the place, although I like the place just fine. I love it how everyone knows everyone. They're like one big family."

"That's OK if you don't mind having someone around all the time."

"Hey, I'm Italian. We love company. Your grandfather is priceless. He's like the way I remember my grandfather."

"I didn't think there was anybody else like Napper but I suppose all grandfathers are alike in some ways especially to their grandchildren."

"Everyone wants to be around him. We were the same with Papa."

"He's something else, for sure. Nobody else gets into Christmas like Napper. You'll see when you spend more time with him. Him and Nan want us to go over for dinner tomorrow. That's what you call lunch."

"What do people around here call dinner?"

"Supper."

"I see. I think. Anyway, that's better for us. We won't have to keep Laura up late."

"That, my sweet, is why Nan figured lunch would be best. One thing I can promise you is that you'll never meet two people who are more in love than the two of them. Honest to God, they're like teenagers."

"Are you serious?"

"You'll see for yourself as you get to know them better." He put his arms around her, pulled her up on his chest, and kissed her. "Right now you and I should start trying to catch up with them."

The next day Gina and Jim bundled little Laura in her red and white bunting suit and bought her to her great-grandparent's home. Right away the little one fell for Napper and Bertha. First, pictures had to be taken with both of them and then with each individually. Bertha gave the child beautiful red and green Christmas mitts and then brought Gina to tears with a matching pair for her. Of course, it being his first great-grandchild and Christmas too, Napper had made the extra effort, but he should have waited until they finished eating before he showed it to Laura. It was the finest dancing master that he had ever made. Carved and painted to look like a toy soldier with a polished black hat and bright red coat, he had big red cheeks and wore a smile from ear to ear. Napper said the smile was because his boots were built for dancing, not marching. Napper had a stick about a foot long fixed to the toy's back. With a bit of practice one could hold the dancer on a table or chair and by tapping the stick make him to out-dance the best step-dancers in John's Pond. Laura laughed hard as Napper made the little soldier dance. She tried to dance as fast as the toy and squealed in protest when her great-grandfather paused to eat some of the baked cod that Bertha had served for lunch.

After they were all finished eating Napper and Jim played with Laura while Gina and Bertha talked. The afternoon flew quickly and soon it was time for Jim to bring his wife and baby back to his father's house. Before they left, however, Napper instructed Jim to get the hand-cat from the shed and pull it to the top of the meadow so Gina and Laura could have a ride. Napper and Bertha watched from their kitchen window. The laughter of the young family told them that the passage of time had changed nothing to dampen the appeal of the big sled.

Too soon, it was time for Jim and his family to return to Toronto. They visited Napper and Bertha again the evening before their departure to say good-bye. Laura sat on her great-grandfather's knee and played with her dancing master. Gina and Jim were enjoying Bertha's dark fruitcake when Gina raised an idea that hadn't crossed anyone's mind.

"I loved every minute I was here," she said. "I'm going to miss everyone, especially you and Napper. I'd love it if both of you would come to Toronto and spend next Christmas with us."

"Oh my heavens," Bertha said, "we'd never be able to do that at our age."

"Why not?" Jim said. " Laura was able to make it at her age."

"God love her," Bertha said with a smile to the child on Napper's lap, "but we've never been on an airplane."

"All the more reason to go," Gina said.

"That's true," Napper said.

"Then you'll do it?" Gina said, delight evident on her face.

"Oh, I never said that," Napper said. "That's too much to agree to without thinking it over a spell."

"But you're not saying no? Are you?"

Napper laughed and hugged the little girl in his lap. "No, we're not saying no, either. We'll see what happens over the summer."

That's how it started. Jim and Gina told everyone that Napper and Bertha were thinking about travelling to Toronto to spend a Christmas in the city. It's fair to say that disbelief was first reaction from most everyone at the notion of Napper and Bertha spending Christmas anywhere but John's Pond. But when Napper stated that there was really no reason they couldn't go that folks began to think that the trip might take place. Ned Keefe provided the final shove.

BUON NATALE

Just after St. Patrick's Day Napper's old friend wasn't feeling well and made a trip to Placentia hospital for a check up. Napper walked over to his house after supper to see how he made out. He knew as soon as he saw Kitty's face that things had not gone well.

"It's not good," Ned said as they sat to the kitchen table. "They tell me they can give me some treatments but it'll only buy me a bit more time."

"Maybe it's not as bad as they think," Napper said. "The doctors aren't always right."

"I expect they're right this time. I've known for a while that something is amiss inside but I never had the gumption to go see about it. You know something though? I got no regrets." Napper stared as his friend continued. "Don't get me wrong; I'd love to have a few more years but I've had a good life and I've done pretty well everything I wanted to. I can't ask for more than that."

"I suppose that's all any of us can ask for," Napper said. "It's probably a lot easier to accept whatever is ahead of us if we can look back with no regrets."

Napper stayed with Ned and Kitty for hours. They talked about the days of their youth, their children and how to face the days ahead. One thing became clear to Napper and Kitty as the night wore on—Ned was a contented man who was able to accept whatever fate held for him. Napper took his time walking home. He thought about everything they talked about. Bertha was waiting up for him. She was stunned by the news about Ned. An hour later, as they sat to the kitchen table, Napper looked at her over the rim of the teacup at his lips.

"We're going to take that trip to Toronto this Christmas," he said.

"Why are you thinking about that now?"

"Ned says that when all is said and done we have to be able to look back and have no regrets. He's in a position to know what he's talking about. This year, if we are spared, we'll be married fifty years. We're going to take that honeymoon we never had back then."

Ned didn't last long. He was gone by the end of June. Napper took his friend's passing hard but it steeled his resolve about the trip. Two weeks after Ned's funeral he had Joey drive him to St. John's. He came back with two round trip tickets to Toronto. They were leaving on Friday, December 18th.

Napper was up three o'clock in the morning. By three-thirty he had breakfast cooked for Bertha and their bags put out in the porch. She was dressed to go when she came downstairs. Napper couldn't help but stare at her. Her blond hair had long been replaced by silver and hints of lines showed on her face, but her eyes, her voice, her graceful movements were the same as those of the young woman he fell in love with so long ago. In his eyes age had taken nothing from her.

Before they finished breakfast they heard tires scrunching on snow as Mike backed his car in the lane. He loaded his parents bags into the trunk before he came into the kitchen.

"Cup of tea?" Napper asked.

"No, I had one before I left the house. So, you two are sure you want to do this?"

"My love, we were never so sure of anything in our lives," Bertha said.

"Well then, we better get on the way."

Moments later they had the house secured and they pulled out of the yard. The houses of John's Pond were dark and silent as the car passed and turned on to the road to St. John's. They spent the first few minutes of the drive questioning each other to make sure they had taken everything: the airline tickets, money, and gifts— even though they had re-checked everything dozens of times in the previous days. Mike then listened patiently while Bertha re-minded him again about caring for the house and animals.

"Mom, the house and the horse and the hens will all be here when you get back. You and Dad just think about enjoying yourselves."

"I know. It's just that we've never been away for so long before."

"The time will fly. Before you know it I'll be going back to the airport to bring you home."

"I suppose Jim won't forget to pick us up in Toronto."

Mike laughed. "That's something you definitely don't have to worry about. Judging from his letters, he's probably already at the airport. Him and Gina are pretty eager to see you."

"No more eager than we are to see them and little Laura," Napper said. "I dare say she's all grown up now."

Two hours later they pulled into the parking lot at Torbay air-port on the outskirts of St. John's. Inside travellers bustled about while the public address system blared with announcements of ar-rivals and departures. Mike and Napper carried the luggage to the Trans Canada Airlines counter. A smiling young lady examined their tickets.

"Good morning, Mr. and Mrs. Darby. You have a beautiful day for your flight to Toronto."

"I'm so excited," Bertha said. "We've never been on an airplane before."

"I'm sure you will enjoy it. We take good care of our passengers. "

"What time will we land in Toronto?" Napper asked.

"At three pm Toronto time. That's four-thirty here."

"I didn't know the trip would take so long," Bertha said.

"You will be landing in Halifax and Montreal so you can get off the airplane if you want to and stretch your legs. Breakfast will be served between here and Halifax and you will have a nice lunch between Halifax and Montreal."

"Well now, I'm starting to like this flying business already," Napper said.

The ticket lady laughed as she labelled their luggage and put it on a conveyor belt. "Your flight will be boarding at about five forty-five and taking off at six. We'll announce it over the public address system. Have a wonderful trip."

"Thank you very much," Bertha said.

Mike waited with his parents until the flight was announced and then accompanied them across the tarmac to the steps of the huge four-engine plane. He shook hands with his father and hugged his mother. "Have a safe trip and enjoy yourselves. Give Laura a big hug for me."

"We will," said Bertha as she started up the steps ahead of Napper. A smartly dressed stewardess waited for them at the top of the steps and directed them to seats near the back. A few minutes after they were buckled into their seats the engines came to life. Bertha squeezed Napper's hand as the propellers raced into a blur and the airplane began to move. They listened attentively while the stewardess went through the safety demonstrations.

"Oh my, I hope we don't need any of that stuff."

"They're just being careful," Napper said.

The airplane turned at the end of the runway and stood still for a few seconds. Then the engines roared and Napper and Bertha were pressed back in their seats as the airplane raced down the runway. "Here we go," Napper said. Seconds later they were airborne.

"I can't believe we did it," Bertha said. They gazed out the window as the ground fell away beneath them.

Napper and Bertha delighted in every part of the flight. A cheerful young stewardess served them a delicious ham and eggs breakfast. In Halifax they got off the plane and took a stroll through the terminal before continuing on to Montreal. En route to Montreal they had a lunch of roast turkey. They had only just finished when they landed. The plane had to be refuelled so Napper and Bertha had almost two hours to explore Montreal airport. Many of the people spoke French; the few who did speak English did so with a thick accent. Napper and Bertha were charmed by it. They discovered a café in the terminal that served delectable pastries and coffee with the most wonderful aroma. They rested there, savouring everything around them. Soon they re-boarded the airplane for the final leg of their flight. They watched the cities, towns, lakes and rivers pass below them. In a little over an hour they began to descend. The huge city stretched as far as they could see.

"I never thought a place could be so big," Napper said peering out the airplane windows.

"This is what it looks like when hundreds of thousands of people live in one place," she said. "I hope Jim is waiting for us. We'll never find our own way around a place that big."

After making a few steep turns the airplane glided to a smooth landing and stopped in front of the terminal building. Napper spotted Jim soon as he stepped inside the building. Gina and Laura were with him. Broad smiles crossed their faces.

"Welcome to Toronto," Jim said. He held Laura in one arm while he hugged Bertha and then Napper with the other. The child was no longer the baby that her great-grandparents met a year earlier. She had grown into a raven-haired beauty with huge brown eyes.

"Oh, aren't you the image of your mommy!" Bertha said. The little girl was a bit apprehensive for a moment but after watching her dad hug Napper and Bertha she was quick to warm them again. Napper extended his arms to her. She smiled and allowed him and Bertha to plant a kiss on her cheeks. Napper was the first to notice Gina's swollen belly.

"Well, what's this? Either you've been eating real good or little Laura is going to have a baby brother or sister."

"In about another two months," Gina said, laughing and rubbing her belly, "but I wish we already had him—or her."

"This is wonderful," Bertha said. "I can help you with Laura and you'll be able to get some rest."

"Nan, we didn't get you and Napper to come all this way to go to work. We want you to see the sights and enjoy yourselves. Now, let's get your luggage and get out of here."

Soon they were in the car and pulling away from the airport. Napper twisted and turned from one side to the other to scrutinise the towering buildings lining the streets.

"They like to build them high around here, don't they?"

"These are tiny," Jim said. "Wait until you see some of the towers downtown." A half-hour later they were in an older section of the city where shops and restaurants replaced the office and apartment buildings. "This is Little Italy. Nan, you'll love the stuff in the stores around here. You won't find any of it in Thistle's store back home."

"Do you live far from here?" Bertha asked.

"We're almost there. We just moved into a house by a playground off College Street." Jim said.

"It's only a few blocks from my parents' house," Gina said.

Five minutes later Jim pulled onto a street lined with rows of townhouses. He stopped in front of one. "Here we are—home sweet home. What do you think?"

"Looks like a fine spot," Napper said, as he scanned the houses standing shoulder to shoulder on the other side of the sidewalk, "providing you get along with the neighbours."

"It's not as bad as you would think," Jim said. "Everyone respects everyone else's space. Most of the people around here are really nice when you get to know them."

"Most people everywhere are nice when you get to know them," Napper said.

"Oh my, this is beautiful," Bertha said when Gina led them inside the house. Jim followed with their luggage. The house was bright and, Bertha noticed, spotless. Flowers decorated the tables and a beautiful Christmas tree stood in the corner of the living room.

"We haven't put any gifts under it yet because Laura doesn't understand that she has to wait until Christmas morning to open them," Gina said. "I have your room all ready. Jim, bring your grandparents' cases upstairs." She led Bertha up the stairs.

Jim winked at his grandfather. "See what happens Napper when we get indoors. She takes right over and starts giving orders."

"Get used to it, young fellow. I've been saying 'yes ma'am' for more than fifty years."

"Oh, my goodness, this is lovely," Bertha said as she followed Gina into the bedroom. The young woman's careful preparations were evident. Sunlight streamed in through the large window showing off a vase of carnations on a dresser. The bed was covered with a quilt that Bertha knew had to be handcrafted. A welcoming rose lay on each pillow.

"You like it?" Jim asked as he and Napper entered the room. "Gina's been getting it ready for weeks."

"It shows," Bertha said. She opened her arms, pulled Gina to her and kissed her on the cheek. "This is about the nicest thing anyone has ever done for us. You're a sweetheart. Thank you."

"I wanted to treat you as good as you treated us last year," Gina said.

"My darling, you've already done that and more," Napper said. He turned to Jim. "You look after this girl. You're lucky to have her. She's a keeper."

"I figured that out a long time ago," Jim said.

"I'll help you unpack," Gina said, "and then you can have a little rest after your trip. My parents are coming over later on to meet you."

"Oh, that will be nice," Bertha, said, "but I can handle unpacking myself. You can look after Laura."

"Jim and Napper can keep Laura busy. Jim, take Laura downstairs and I'll help your grandmother. You can show Napper around the rest of the house."

"Come on Napper. We got our orders." He picked up Laura and turned the stairs. Napper followed him. "Are you going to show Napper the Christmas tree?" he asked Laura. She nodded. He put her down at the bottom of the stairs. She ran to the Christmas tree.

"See, see the tree and the Ceppo." She laughed and jumped as she spoke.

"Well now, that is a pretty tree," Napper said. "And what did you call this thing?" Napper pointed to a wooden pyramid frame about five feet high, with shelves. The bottom shelf held a beautiful nativity scene. The whole thing was decorated with coloured paper and pinecones. A star shone from the top.

"It's our Ceppo. It's pretty."

"It is pretty. Did your mommy put all this stuff on it?"

"Uh huh,"

"Did you help her?"

Laura nodded. Napper turned his attention to the tree. "This is a pretty nice tree too. What's Santa Claus going to put underneath it?"

"Dolls and a red bike and candy and a doll house and, and … other stuff."

"What other stuff?"

"Dolls and a red bike and a doll house and lots of stuff, right daddy?"

"That's right, sweetheart and who else will leave something for you?"

"La Befana!"

"La Befana, that's right."

"Who is La Befana?" Napper asked.

"Tell Napper who La Befana is."

"Nice old witch!"

Jim saw his grandfather's puzzlement and offered an explanation. "La Befana is a kind witch who brings things to Italian children on January 6th—what we've always called Old Christmas Day. The story is that the three wise men stopped at her hut to ask directions and wanted her to go along with them but she refused. A shepherd is supposed to have stopped and wanted her to go with him too, but she said 'no'. Then she changed her mind and took some toys belonging to a child of her own who had died and set out after the wise men. Italians say she's been roaming the world ever since looking for the Christ Child and leaving gifts for children. Gina and I figured it was important for Laura to know about it and to put up a Ceppo."

"Isn't that something?" Napper said. "I never heard of it before." He reached down and tickled Laura's chin. "You're going to have to tell Nan all about that nice old witch. I thought they only came around on Halloween."

"La Befana is the Christmas witch," Laura said. "She's a nice witch."

Jim watched with delight as the bond strengthened between the child and her great-grandfather. He put his hand on Napper's shoulder. "You're going to love some of the stuff that Italians do at Christmas. Wait until you see the crib they have built in the church. It's unbelievable."

"That'll be good to see. I might get a few ideas for the one I have back home or give them a few pointers about how I build 'em."

Jim directed Napper to an armchair in the corner of the living room opposite the Christmas tree. "I'll put on a pot of coffee while Gina and Nan are unpacking and putting away your stuff upstairs."

"Ah now, that sounds grand," Napper said as he lowered himself into the armchair. "What did you do with the dancing master I made for the little one last Christmas?"

"It's right there." Jim pointed to a shelf near the tree. "Everyone who comes in wants to know what it is and where we got it. Laura would play with it around the clock if we let her. Laura, do you want to show Napper how the dancing master works?"

"OK." She ran to get the little wooden man from her father. "Watch him." She held the toy above the coffee table so his feet could dance to her taps on the support handle.

Napper laughed and clapped his hands to Laura's delight. "Can you dance as good as he can?" Laura shook her head. "Then I'll have to show you."

"Show her what?" Bertha asked, as she and Gina appeared on the stairs.

"I'm going to show her how to dance."

"My love, he'll only step on your toes," Bertha said to Laura. "You let your mommy and daddy teach you how to dance."

For the next hour Napper and Bertha chatted with Jim and Gina. As one might expect, Laura was the centre of attention. Gina eventually had to excuse herself to tend to the evening meal.

Bertha then suggested to Napper that a little rest might be in order before they met Gina's parents. He agreed and they went back upstairs. Both were wearier than they realised and fell asleep almost immediately. The nap did them good. They felt refreshed when Jim tapped on the bedroom door and hour later to announce that the meal was almost ready to be served. They made their way downstairs just as a large car stopped in front of the house. Laura pulled the curtain aside to see the car and then ran squealing to the door.

"Papa, Nana!" The little girl tugged at the knob in a futile effort to open the door.

"Wait, wait sweetheart. Mommy will get it for you." Gina hustled to the door as fast as her rotund condition would allow. She opened it and hugged a well-dressed couple as they entered. "Buon Natale, Mamma. Buon Natale, Papa."

"Buon Natale, sweetheart," the man said, planting a kiss on Gina's cheek. The affection between them was obvious.

"Buon Natale, my baby," the woman said as she kissed Gina and patted her belly.

Gina waited while they hung their coats in the closet and then took their hands to lead them into the living room. "Mamma and Papa, I want you to meet the wonderful people that I've been telling you about all year. This is Jim's grandmother, Bertha Darby, and his grandfather, Napper." She then spoke to Napper and Bertha. "These are my parents, Frank and Maria Caboto."

Napper and Bertha shook hands with Frank and Maria.

"Welcome to Toronto," Frank said. "We're delighted to finally meet you."

"Gina has talked about you constantly since her trip to Newfoundland," his wife said. "I've been looking forward to you coming here as much as she has. How was your trip?"

"It was lovely, ma'am," Napper said. "It was our first ride on an airplane and it was wonderful."

"I thought I might be nervous," Bertha said, "but I can't wait to do it again."

Gina steered them all towards the sofa and armchairs. "Dinner will be ready in just a couple of minutes."

"I'll help you," her mother said.

"Yes, you sit down and rest," Bertha said, getting to her feet. "I can help with the food."

Gina laughed and held up her hands to stop both of them. "I want all of you to sit down and get acquainted. Jim and I have the meal under control." She picked up her daughter and placed her in Frank's arms. "Laura, will stay here with you so you have something to talk about."

Frank was a soft-spoken, thoughtful man who had spent his life in the fast-paced construction industry of the big city. His wife was more outgoing but the centre of her universe was their family. The four of them were getting into the similarities of their families when Jim announced that dinner was ready.

He seated them around the table where Gina proceeded to serve a delicious antipasto seafood salad followed by fettuccine with smoked salmon. Napper could hardly believe when she explained that these were only appetizers. The main dish was *baccala*, a dried salted cod dish.

"Now that I am familiar with," Napper said, "but you have it dressed up a lot more than my way of doing it."

"How do you prepare it?" Gina asked.

"Well now, let me tell you about a feed that myself and Will Kerrivan put together the night young Jim's father was born." Napper then proceed to regale all of them with tales of John's Pond from years long gone. Frank responded with stories from the Italy of his childhood. The meal and the conversation went on for hours. Napper and Bertha took a great liking to Frank and Maria and it was obvious that Gina's parents enjoyed the company of their new-found friends just as much. At the end of the night

Maria Caboto asked Napper and Bertha about their plans for the next few nights.

"We have no plans, my dear," Bertha said. "We'll do whatever Jim and Gina want to do."

"Tomorrow night we are going to a concert of the boys' choir at St. Catherina of Siena's cathedral. It's always a beautiful show. Will you come with us?"

Bertha looked at Napper. Before he could say anything both Jim and Gina spoke up.

"You'll love it," Gina said. "I'd go."

"Me too," Jim said. "It's a concert you'll remember for the rest of your life. I couldn't believe how good it was the first time I heard them. We'd go too only for it would be too long for little Laura. She'd get fussy."

That concert was the beginning of another wonderful Christmas for Napper and Bertha. The beautiful candle-lit cathedral dazzled them while they listened to wonderful carols performed by more than a hundred gifted boys. It was, however, a performance of *The First Noel* that left Napper entranced.

"The first time I heard that song was when Judy Power sang it in the old school house on the hill. When I closed my eyes it was as though I was back there listening to her all over again," he told Bertha as they lay in bed a few hours later.

Gina's family and friends treated them like royalty. Every evening they were guests at lavish Italian meals the likes of which neither of them could even have imagined.

"I never saw so much food in in all my life," Napper said.

"And it's all so good," Bertha said as they watched another course being served at the home of Gina's brother the night before Christmas Eve.

"Christmas is a time of joy to be celebrated," Frank Caboto stated to his new friends. "What better way than with fine food, fine music and wonderful friends? This is where memories are made."

Napper and Bertha were eager for Christmas morning to arrive, almost as eager as little Laura. When the big day came her squeals woke them before dawn. They pulled on their robes and went downstairs.

"Santa was here! Santa was here! Look, I got a bike and a dollhouse. Come see."

"Ah, you'll remember these mornings forever," Napper told Jim as the young man snapped pictures of his happy little girl. Later that afternoon they all went to the home of Gina's parents where Maria Caboto served up two main courses. The first, a huge roasted turkey, she explained was prepared in honour of Napper and Bertha. The second was the traditional Italian Christmas meal, *capitone*, a big baked female eel. Amid cries of encouragement from all around the table Napper tried some first and then Bertha tasted it. Both of them declared that it was delicious.

"Standing on the bridge and watching eels swim upriver will never be the same again," Napper said.

When the meal eventually ended they all made their way to the Caboto's parlour where tea and coffee was served. Young Jim stood in the centre of the room and called for attention. The crowd grew quite as he spoke.

"Since you welcomed me into your family a few years ago I've been telling you stories about John's Pond. Just about all of those stories included my wonderful grandparents, Napper and Nan Darby. Last year Gina and I were able to take Laura to Newfoundland and spend Christmas with our family there. Gina and Laura loved my grandparents as much as all the rest of us have for many years. It was Gina who came up with the idea that they come to Toronto this year. Let me tell you that back home nobody, and I do mean nobody, ever expected them to leave John's Pond at Christmas time. They're as much a part of Christmas back home as hand-cat rides and the mummers. Gina will explain those things to you. Yet, here they are and we are overjoyed that they made the trip"

"Here, here," Frank Caboto said raising his glass to a round of applause from all assembled. The interruption came at a good time. Young Jim was beginning to choke up and needed a moment to gather his composure before going on.

"Nan, Napper, by coming here you gave Gina, Laura and me memories that will last us forever. No matter how long we live or where we go we will always remember this Christmas that you spent with us. With that in mind, Laura wants to give you our gift from us. We put a lot of thought into trying to get something perfect and it all came down to what you seem to always do for everyone else. You give us things to remember. So, Laura, give Napper and Nan their gift and we hope it will be something that they will remember for the rest of their lives."

The little girl ran across the room into her great-grandmothers open arms.

"For you and Napper," she said as she shoved small package into Bertha's hands. Bertha sat back in her armchair with Laura snuggled tight to her and began to unwrap the gift. Inside the package was an envelope and inside the envelope was two small cardboard slips. Bertha stared at them for a few seconds before she realized what she was holding.

"Oh my, Napper! It's tickets to a hockey game. We're going to see the Maple Leafs and the Canadiens. We're going to Maple Leaf Gardens."

Napper took the tickets from Bertha and stared at them. His face couldn't hold a bigger smile. "This is something I only dreamed about. We're going to get to see all the stuff that we've been hearing on the radio. Oh my, I wish Ned was still alive so I could tell him about this when we get home." He hugged Gina first and then Jim. "How did you ever know what to get us?"

"How did we know?" Jim's smile was almost as wide as Napper's. "How could I ever forget the crowds in your front room Saturday nights listening to the games on the radio? Nan, you were into it just as much as Napper and Ned and the rest of them. I thought it would be something both of you would remember."

"You couldn't have done better," Bertha said. She steered little Laura to Napper and proceeded to hug Gina and Jim. "You couldn't have given us a better gift."

Four nights later Napper and Bertha along with Gina's parents, who as it turned out were the ones who actually managed to come up with the tickets to the sold-out game, went to watch the Toronto Maple Leafs and their arch rivals, the Montreal Canadiens, battle to a 1-1 tie. Montreal's great Rocket Richard scored his 401st goal late in the first period. With five minutes left in the game Richard got into a fight with one of the Leafs and the same fans who cheered in the first period laid a barrage of boos on him. Napper and Bertha loved every minute of it.

"I have a hard time saying anything good about the Canadiens but I have to hand it to Richard," Napper said after the game, "he makes things happen. I'll give him that much."

"I thought it was all wonderful," Bertha said. "Now when I listen to the games on the radio I'll be able to see it all in my mind."

Napper and Bertha didn't stop for the whole Christmas season. They took in the sights of the city, shopped at the legendary Eaton's department store and went with Jim, Gina and Laura to a photographer's studio to have portraits done. The photographer even arranged to have the pictures shipped home for them. Too soon, the time came for them to pack and return home. Saying good-bye to so many new friends was harder than they expected. Gina's mother summed it up best.

"We never know when we will see each other again but it is something we can always look ahead to. In the meantime we must be grateful for having met and the time we spent together. It has made all of our lives richer."

Lying in bed a few hours before their flight home Bertha turned to Napper. "Taking this trip was one of the smartest things we ever did. I wish everyone could get around and see how wonderful the world is. I can't wait to tell the crowd back home all about it."

CHRISTMAS ALL AGLOW

One March morning in 1961 Bertha sat across the breakfast table and stared at Napper.

"What are you looking at?" he asked.

"All the white hair on your head. I believe you're getting old."

"I find myself thinking the same thing every time I look in the mirror, and you know something, I don't think it's fair for that to be happening to me while you stay the same as you did the first day I met you."

She stood up and walked to the stove to refill her teacup. On the way she patted him on the head. "One of the things I always loved about you is that you were never much of a liar."

After breakfast she washed the dishes and got ready to make bread. He put on his coat and cap and set out on foot to the post office. His truck was there to use but he said the walk was good for him and he was in no hurry. Bertha was surprised when less than half an hour later she saw him coming in the road at a brisk pace. He would normally do away with the best part of the morning before he came back. "There must be nobody left alive for him to talk to."

He came through the porch and on into the kitchen without even stopping to take off his coat. He had a smile from ear to ear. "You'd never believe what I just heard."

"It must be something good. What is it?"

"They're putting the lights through here."

"Are you sure?"

"There's a power company truck parked up by the post office. I was talking to them myself. They're hiring fellows today to start cutting right-of-ways for the poles. They said they'll have the lines strung and the power on before Christmas."

"Oh my. Are you sure?"

"That's what the men in the truck just told me not ten minutes ago."

"I can't believe we're finally going to have lights at the flick of a switch."

"Not just lights. You can get electric washers and irons, even toasters and kettles. We'll be able to get our breakfast without even having to make the fire. Bertha my darling, we're going to have the life of royalty."

"I suppose you're even going to get one of those electric blankets to keep me warm, aren't you."

He stepped up behind her, wrapped his arms around her and lifted her off the floor. "Now that's something we'll never need. I've kept you warm all these years and I'm not letting any light bulb take that job."

She laughed as she wiggled her way back to the floor and turned around to kiss him. "You're getting older but you never did grow up."

No little boy ever followed a hockey or baseball team through the season with the enthusiasm that Napper watched the progress of the power company crews. Every evening he made it a point to chat with some of the men working on the right-of-way to learn how far they had come. He could scarcely contain himself in August when the work of sticking the poles began, leaving no doubt but the project was for real. A couple of times a week he started up his pick-up truck and travelled in along Whitbourne road to see exactly where they were. The line crews soon got to know him and invited him to join them during their breaks. He was having a cup of coffee with them by St. Shore's pond in early September when one of the men made a comment that got Napper thinking.

"Don't you worry, skipper," the linesman said. "You're safe enough buying Christmas lights this year. You put them up and we'll put the juice to them."

Napper spent much of his time for the rest of September and early October in his shed. When Bertha inquired as to what he was up to he assured her that he was fixing up the nativity crib and some other Christmas stuff to pass away the time. She thought it nothing strange when Napper told her one Friday evening that Mike was driving the pick-up to St. John's on Saturday and he was going along for the ride. When they returned on Saturday evening, however, and Mike backed the truck up to Napper's shed door she knew something was up—especially when Joey and Billy showed up minutes later and she could hear them all laughing. She pulled on her coat and tied a bandanna around her head. The shed was Napper's domain and she was usually content to leave him alone there but now her curiosity got the better of her. Her jaw dropped when she opened the shed door.

"What in heaven's name is all of this?"

"Just those Christmas things I told you I was working on."

"You told me you were fixing up the nativity crib."

"I said I was doing some other stuff too."

"Mom, you mean to say you didn't know about all this?" Billy asked.

"Indeed, I didn't. What is it all anyway?" By then her three sons were all laughing heartily as they looked at the satisfied grin on Napper's face.

He made his way to the shed door and took her by the arm. "Come in my love and look at what I have ready for our first Christmas with lights. Right here beside you is a star."

"I can see that. What are you going to do with it?"

"I have it rigged for lights and I'm going to put it up on a pole over the nativity crib. I got that all set up for lights too, even the manger."

"What's all the rest of it?"

"Over there is Santa Claus and his sleigh and the reindeer. I'm going to put a light in the front fellow's nose and paint it red just like in that song I hear on the radio."

"Rudolph," Joey said.

"That's the one. This stuff is a gingerbread house like the ones you make for the youngsters. All I have to do is bring it out, put it together and put in the lights."

"Where are you getting all the lights?"

"I got them today in St. John's." He pointed to the pile of boxes and bags lying on the floor. "I got enough to go around every window in the front of the house and right around the eves."

"He got the Christmas spirit this year, mom." Mike said.

"He's always had plenty of that. It's one of the things I love the most about him." She looked at the broad smile on his face and matched it with one of her own as she hugged him.

"You love me for more reasons than that, don't you?" he said.

"Never mind that. Are you going to have time to get all of this up after we get the power? I heard it mightn't be turned on until just before Christmas."

"My darling, I'm starting to put this up tomorrow. It's going to be in place and plugged in so when the power comes on this is the first thing that'll be lit up in John's Pond."

That's just the way it happened. The switch was thrown on Wednesday evening, December 20th. Everyone in the place came out to walk or drive the roads and marvel that the darkness was finally driven out of John's Pond, but it was the Darby home that set the standard. Along with the light streaming from the windows and from the bulb over the porch door, the property was a crescendo of colour. Rudolph glowed from the fence by the driveway. The windows and rooftop were outlined with twinkling coloured bulbs. The nativity crib radiated with brilliance from the front garden and above it shone a star that would have made the three wise men shade their eyes. Looking back, it wasn't a lot compared to some of the gaudy displays we see today but it was a marvel at the time. The light of the Christmas Man shone for all to see.

SHINING STARS IN THE SKY

The July sun warmed Napper's back as he made his way to the hen-house early one morning in 1968. He let out the hens into the yard and then gathered the eggs and brought them back to the kitchen. He filled the kettle, put it on the electric range and sat down to wait for it to boil. Bertha moved overhead. Moments later he thought he heard her call his name. He went to the bottom of the stairs.

"Did you say something?"

No response.

He started up the stairs. "I have the kettle on. It'll be boiled in a few minutes."

Still no answer.

"I have some fresh eggs for breakfast. Do you want…" His voice trailed off at the sight of her in the bed. "Oh no, no. Bertha, what's wrong?"

She had to work hard to speak. "Come, come close."

He bent over the bed and clasped her hand in his. "What's wrong? I'll get some help."

"No. Stay here with me." He could hardly hear her.

"I don't know what to do. Tell me what to do."

"There's nothing to do. We can't stop it." She saw the panic in his face. "Listen to me."

"I am listening. Tell me what you want."

"When they take me to the church I want you to look at our children and their children. Look at all of them. You and me... we're part of all of them."

"Don't go! Please, not yet."

A smile crossed her face. "It's like...it all lasted no longer than... than a dream. Hold me like you always do. You...you kept ...you kept your promise."

Bertha was buried on one of the hottest days of the summer. They came from far and wide; friends, neighbours, children, grandchildren and great-grandchildren filled the church to say good-bye and to support Napper. He spoke to all of them and didn't shed a tear. When the rites in the graveyard ended his family gathered around him.

"We'll take you back to the house when you're ready, Dad," Minnie said.

"Not yet. You can go back. I'll be along shortly. I have to do something." He looked at Minnie's youngest daughter. "Cathy, will you help your old grandfather?"

She took his hand, "Anything you want, Napper. Just tell me."

"I need you to drive me in the road a little ways that new car of yours. Not far."

Cathy looked at her mother.

"Where are you going, dad?" Minnie asked.

"There's a place I have to go. You can come if you like."

Cathy held open the door of her car for Napper to sit in the passenger seat and then took her seat behind the wheel. She expertly guided the Chevy Biscayne out of the cemetery and on to the dirt road. She glanced in her rear-view mirror and smiled. "They're all following us."

He nodded. "I expected they would. This is a nice car. You're a nurse, aren't you?"

"Yeah."

"Do you like it?"

"I love it."

"Good. That's important. Slow down, now. We're almost there." Three or four minutes later pointed to the shoulder of the road. "Stop here. This is it." He got out of the car and walked along the road.

Cathy sat in the car and watched him for a minute. She took note of his bent frame and slow step. She knew that her beloved grandfather had become a very old man. She got out of her car and walked up behind him. "What's so special about this place? There's nothing here."

"It all started here." He turned and smiled at her. Tears were running down his face. He put his hand on her shoulder and pointed to a marsh off to his right. "That's the path to Billy-Boy pond." By then half a dozen more cars were parked and most of his family had joined him and Cathy. They were silent as he spoke. "It was a grand day—just like today. She walked out the road right here and called to me. Imagine if I hadn't gone trouting that morning. I was the luckiest man alive."

Napper didn't have to live alone. All of his family asked, even begged, him to come live with them. He declined. "I still have my health and strength so there's no need for any of you to be tending on me."

He was comfortable enough. He rose every morning at the sound of the rooster crowing and fried blood puddings and eggs for his breakfast. One of Joey's boys had wired the house for electric heat so staying warm was as easy as flicking the thermostat.

His old age pension cheque from the government was plenty to pay the light bill and buy the few things he needed. Other than breakfast he never cooked. Elizabeth or Minnie came every morning to bring his mail and stayed to fix his lunch. Most afternoons at least one or two of his buddies dropped in for a chat about what was right and wrong with the world. It seemed that every evening someone invited him out for supper. A game of cards, followed by a cup of tea passed away the nights until it was time to make his way home to bed. If the weather was miserable especially as the summer turned down into fall and he didn't feel like going out, he watched a bit of television, although he never got fond of it. He figured Jed Clampett was the most sensible fellow to be seen on it.

Yes, no doubt he was comfortable enough. The trouble was, no matter how brave a face he put on, he missed Bertha and it took a toll on him. He never complained, but everyone close to him could see it. Sometimes he was preoccupied—like his mind was somewhere else. He wasn't as quick to laugh and he often sat back and listened to conversations instead of joining in. That wasn't like Napper. One thing did perk him up though—the space flights.

They fascinated him. He couldn't be pried away from the television during a launch or one of the splashdowns. He knew the names of all the astronauts and could explain in detail what the mission did and what was planned for the next one. Knowing this Minnie wasn't at all surprised at his response when she asked him how he wanted to spend Christmas Eve.

"We'll go to the church on Christmas morning. The astronauts are going around the moon on Christmas Eve and I want to stay home and watch it."

"Dad, you know you're not staying home by yourself on Christmas Eve."

"I suppose that wouldn't be right, would it?" His face brightened. "How about everyone coming over here? There's nothing like having young ones around to put you in the Christmas spirit and I'll get to see how those fellows make out trying to get to the moon."

I have often wondered how many were at Napper's house that Christmas Eve. They began arriving about two in the afternoon. His own seven sons and daughters were there along with most of their twenty-nine children and their husbands and wives too. Many of his grandchildren now had children of their own; the youngest still had the wrinkles of a new-born. Of course, a crowd draws a crowd so friends and neighbours piled into the house. The kitchen and front room were full. So were the porch and the hallway. They sat on the stairs and leaned against the wood-box. Mike and Billy lit a fire in the drum in the woodshed and many of the men took sanctuary out there. The youngsters took to the meadow with plastic sleds and aluminium snow saucers but the modern technology was discarded when Billy hauled the old hand-cat down from the shed loft and told the young ones try it out. Laughter from the meadow signalled their approval.

A count of all assembled surely would have hit both sides of a hundred and talk about food and drink; they brought enough for an army. There was dark fruitcake and light fruitcake, salad made with potatoes from Joey's garden and salads made with pineapples from Hawaii. There were roast-beef sandwiches and boiled beef soup; peppermint knobs from St. John's and fudge from Ellen's kitchen; moose heart, cod tongues, raisin-duff and rabbit stew; syrup and pop for the young ones, more vigorous stuff for their elders. Napper observed that the horn of plenty had been dumped over his house.

As the food and drink disappeared the music started. Two young fellows, boyfriends of his granddaughters or great granddaughters as far as Napper could tell, brought out guitars. Another young fellow, one of Marg's crowd, had a mandolin. Joey set the pace with his accordion. The floor buckled and bent as dancers stepped to the jigs and reels, step dances and songs. Then about nine o'clock the children gathered by the television started yelling.

"Napper, Napper, the astronauts are coming on. They're going around the moon."

A chair was put in front of the television for Napper and the crowd fell silent as they strained to watch and listen to the three men in the spaceship. The astronauts spoke to the whole world just like they were standing there in Napper's front room. You could have heard a pin drop as the familiar words of Genesis crossed the void of space and the astronauts wished a Merry Christmas to everyone on the good Earth.

"Wow, that was something. What did you think, Napper?"

All eyes turned to him. "It's wonderful. That's what it is, wonderful. It's like a miracle." He stood up to look at the beaming faces around him. "I remember when we had to walk to Whitbourne to send a telegraph message to St. John's. Now we can sit here and listen to men flying around the moon. It's hard to believe how far we've come in one lifetime."

One of the older teens spoke up. "Who wants to go back out on the hill and do some more sliding?" A chorus of voices signalled approval of the idea. It only took a few minutes for most of the younger crowd to don their winter apparel and pile out of the house.

Napper smiled at their enthusiasm. He turned to Joey. "What's it like outside?"

Joey wiped the steam off the window and cupped his hands around his face to peep outside. "Best kind. I can see the stars but it's cold."

"We can rig for the cold." He stood up straight and spoke louder than he had in months. "Tell the young fellows to get a few armfuls of wood from the shed and make a fire in the meadow."

"What have you got in mind?" Joey asked.

"We're going up there."

"Dad," Minnie said, "it's Christmas Eve."

"I know. I'd forgotten how grand a night like tonight can be. Who's coming with me?" He hauled on his boots and heavy parka. Minnie, seeing he wasn't about to change his mind, put a cap on his head and passed him his gloves before donning her own outer wear.

The young fellows had a fine fire blazing on the top of the hill when Napper stepped out of the house. The crowd followed in single file behind him. They plodded up the gentle slope to the crest. The moonlight on the snow allowed them to gaze around John's Pond. Christmas lights twinkled from the houses illuminating the smoke rising from the woodstoves inside. The water on the harbour was black and still, about ready to turn to ice. Napper soon reached where the fire was sending glowing flankers into the Christmas night.

"It's hard to imagine a more perfect night for Christmas Eve," Napper said as his family gathered around him.

"Nights like this are special, Napper." It was his granddaughter Cathy. She made her way to him and kissed him on the cheek. "I'll never forget this one."

"Good. I wanted to come up here so you would remember it. We just saw something wonderful on the television. Imagine, men are up there flying around the moon right now." Their eyes followed his gaze skyward to the thin crescent of the waxing moon. A minute passed before he continued. "In my lifetime we've gone from kerosene lamps and horses to electric lights and rocket ships. One day some of you might get on a rocket and go to the stars, but wherever you go remember where you came from, and remember the peace of this place. People are like fire. We're born; we light up the world and then we're gone. This place, these woods and meadows tie us together across time." He watched their faces in the glow of the fire. All eyes were on him. "Remember this when you remember me; when all is said and done, all we have is each other. Everything else is smoke and embers." He straightened up smiled and smacked his mitts together. "Now, I want all of you to do something for me."

"Anything you want," Cathy said. "What is it?"

"I want to hear *The First Noel*. It's always been my favourite Christmas carol."

That great song has been sung in cathedrals and concert halls around the world but everyone who was there that night will tell you that it was meant to be sung in a cold meadow.

Cathy said it best. "If I looked over my shoulder and saw shepherds I wouldn't have been a bit surprised. I'm sure angels were singing among us."

They didn't stay in the meadow for long. The cold worked its way into their bones in spite of the fire. In twos and threes they made their way back down over the hill to the house. Before he went indoors Napper stopped and looked back to where a few of the older children were enjoying a final ride on the hand-cat. Their laughter rang through the still night.

"You look pleased with yourself," Mike said, as he and Elizabeth stood alongside their father.

"I have good reason to be. How many men can look around at the end of their lives and see what I see tonight? Your mother and I did things right."

Four generations of Darbys shared the joys of Christmas Day. Napper reigned over the feast and then welcomed a parade of visitors to his house that never let up through Christmas night and all Boxing Day.

After supper on the twenty-seventh he was tired and turned in early. Cathy stayed over with him. He told her to go have some fun with others her own age but she insisted saying it was a treat she hadn't had since she was a little girl. The next morning the crowing rooster woke her at daylight. She lay in bed listening for him to stir. The rooster crowed twice more and still no sound came from his room. She got out of bed, pulled on her robe to ward off the morning chill and crossed the hall to his bedroom door. He was in bed, hardly breathing and too weak to speak, but he managed to open his hand for her to hold. A minute later he was gone.

Napper's words in the meadow were repeated often over the next few days. His children, grandchildren and great-grandchildren shared the stories of his life. They talked of Judy Power, Mr. Mike and Mrs. Lizzie. They spoke of Dick Croke, Will and Mae Kerrivan, Ned and Kitty and most of all about him and Bertha. A couple of the youngsters cried when we laid him in the ground beside her, but for most of us gathered on the hill in the biting cold there was no sadness, only a sense of everything being as it should, of having come full circle and seeing a promise kept.

The End

Harold Davis was born in 1958 in Newfoundland, Canada. He grew up in Colinet, a village nestled between the ocean and forest. He has lived and worked in Newfoundland, western Canada and in the arctic. Today he lives by the side of the Salmonier River in Newfoundland. He and his wife have three grown children and a brand new granddaughter.
Follow him at: https://woodpilewriter.wordpress.com